Sister Wendy Beckett

and

Father Kim En Joong

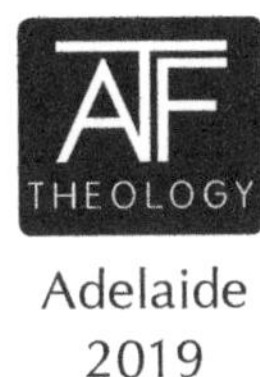

Adelaide
2019

Sister Wendy Beckett

and

Father Kim En Joong

In her words, in his art

The writings by Sr Wendy have been taken from the following publications. Acknowledgment and thanks for the permissions from the originating publishing houses.

Spiritual Letters, Sr Wendy Beckett, London, Bloomsbury, 2013.

Sister Wendy's Bible Treasury, London, Society for Promoting Christian Knowledge, 2012.

Sister Wendy on Prayer, London, Bloomsbury, 2006.

Photo of Sr Wendy by Lou Boileau

Photo of Kim En Joong OP by José Alberto de Blas Moncalvillo

978-1-925872-57-6 paperback
978-1-925872-58-3 hardback
978-1-925872-59-0 epub
978-1-925872-60-6 pdf

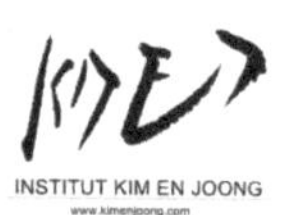

LCT Conseil
7, rue de la Félicité
75017 – Paris
France

Published by:

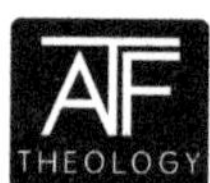

An imprint of the ATF Press Publishing Group owned by ATF (Australia) Ltd.
PO Box 504
Hindmarsh, SA 5007
ABN 90 116 359 963
www.atfpress.com
Making a lasting impact

Dear Sr Wendy,
It is providence that our relationship began. How could I have ever discovered you without by chance finding a book by you in a bookshop in Seoul, Korea? When I saw the portrait of you in this book I did not hesitate to buy it and admire that you were a hermit living in a caravan in the grounds of a Carmelite monastery! I asked myself, how is that you a hermit could present such TV programs on the BBC, something which was quite unimaginable for me!

You were so kind to respond to me when I first wrote to you. We were able to communicate continuously over a long period of time, close on ten years I think.

Happily for me, your community told me of your failing health and I immediately sent you a copy of my latest book, in homage of Cardinal Danneels of Belgium for his 85th birthday. I hope that you were able to contemplate the images and writing in the book before your departure for heaven. It was my publisher, Hilary Regan, who told me of your passing into heaven and so now we are making this book in honour of you with some of your writings and some of my art work.

Your effect has been far and wide across of the oceans in the same way as St Paul the apostle: beyond language, race or age.

Both you and I are as one in a way being outside but contributing to the world. What a beautiful thing that you are in heaven, while I am in the world, but we continue to communicate the beauty for Our Lord.

I wish to thank and acknowledge the various publishers who have allowed me to use your words in this book, my photographer in Paris, Jean-Louis Losi, who always brings out the very best of the colour in my work, Hilary Regan, who collaborates with the Institut Kim En Joong and to all who help me, or have helped me in any way along the way in my artistic career. I thank God for them all. But above all, I thank God, the greatest of all artists, who has given me this gift and who has put all of these people, including you my friend, Sr Wendy, into my life.

Thank you!

Fr Kim En Joong OP
Dominican Convent (Priory) of the Annunciation
Paris, March 2019

The astonishing thing about prayer is our inability to accept that we have need of it, as we do, then because of God's goodness, it cannot be something that is difficult.[1]

1. *On Prayer*, 3.

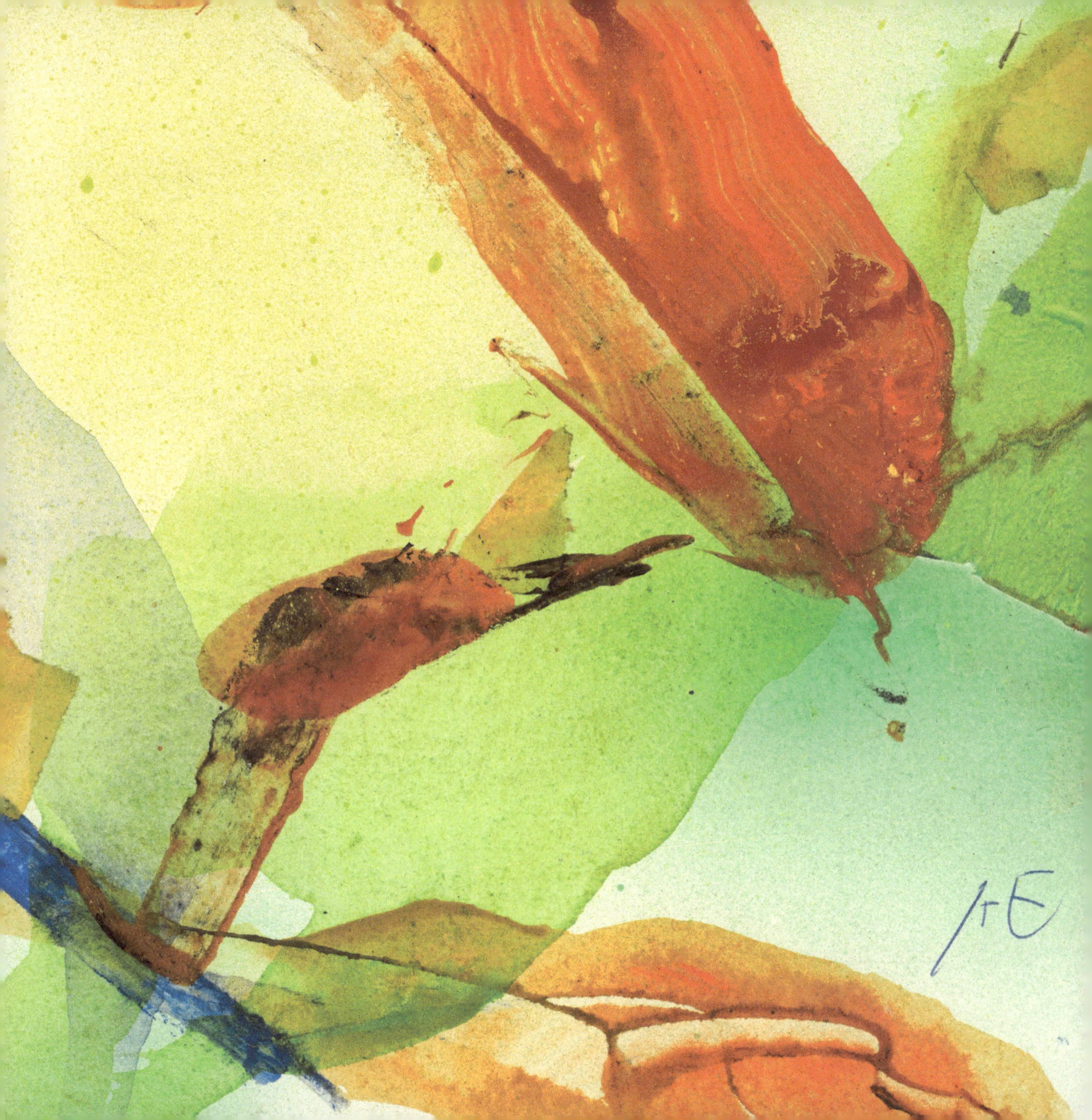

Total trust in God is the only true foundation—we can't afford to live at peace while we inwardly believe all depends on us, and that we hold God's love on the fragile basis of our virtue.[2]

2. *Spiritual Letters*, 297.

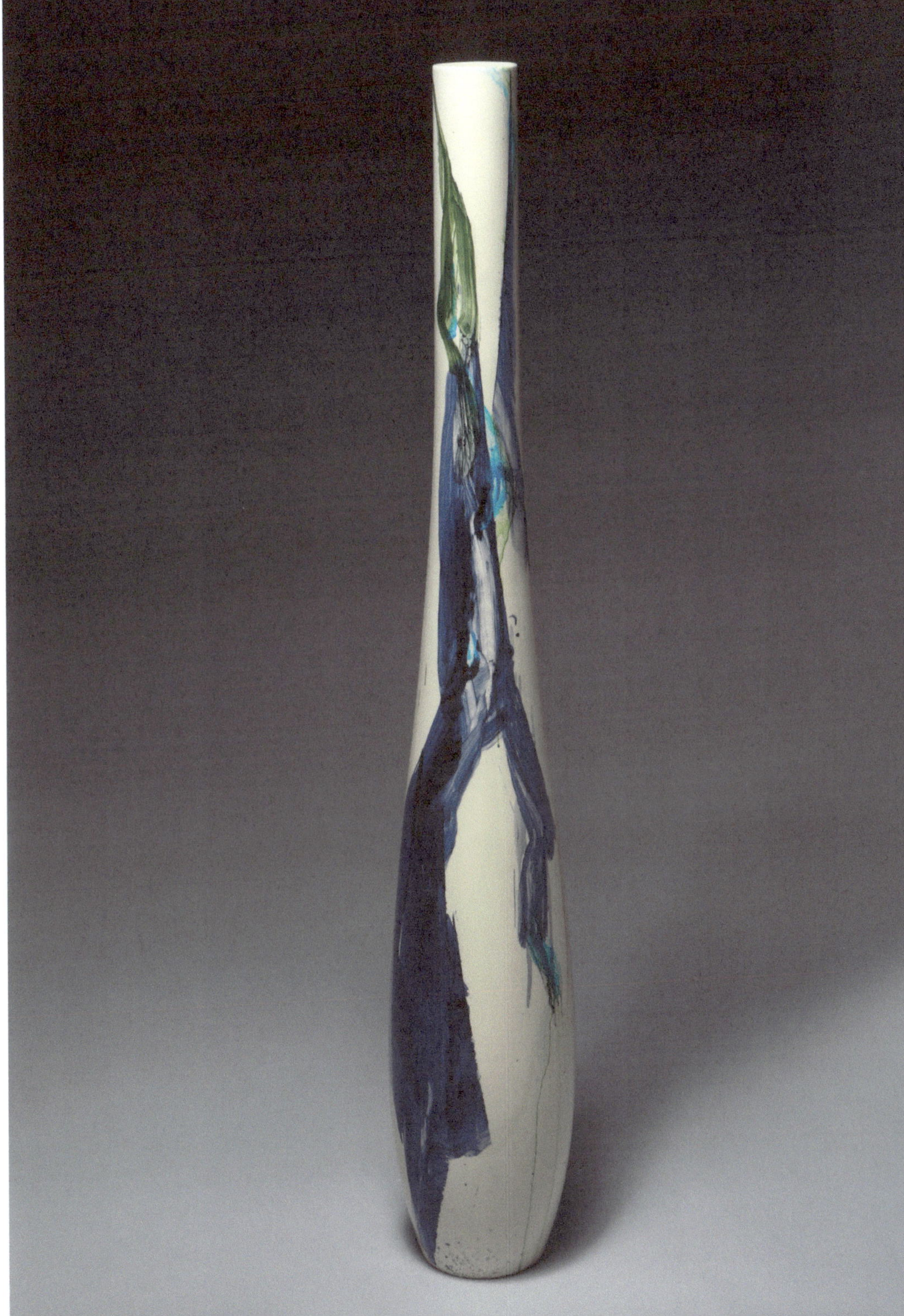

When we pray, we are . . . carried, borne along by a power that we do not and cannot direct. It is our prayer, our boat. It is we who have launched it on to this sea of faith and we who stay quite within it.[3]

3. *On Prayer*, 5–6.

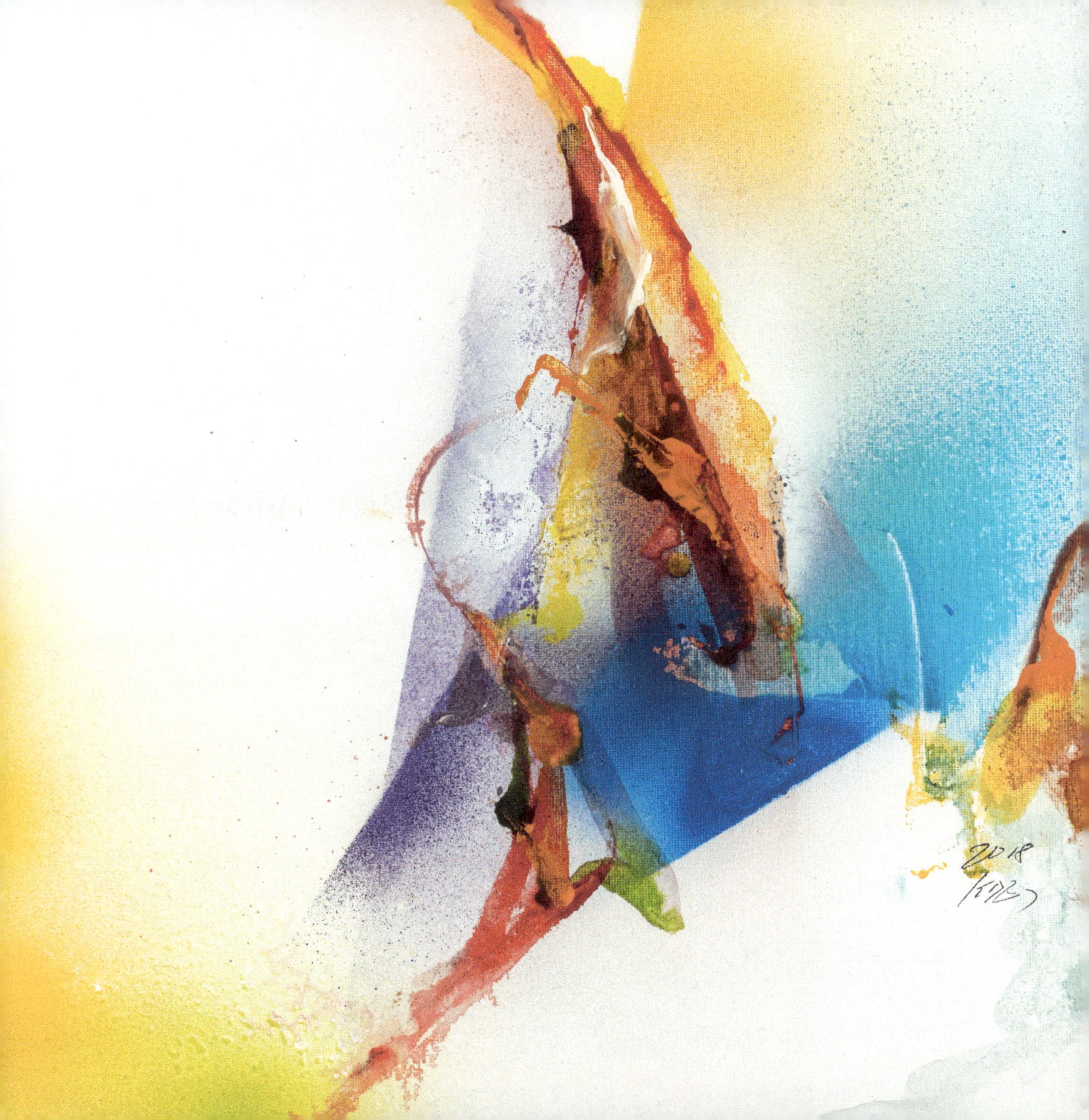

But [in prayer] all the movement comes from God . . . Where we want to go is not to the point; it is where God wants to take us. We do not see where that is.[4]

4. *On Prayer*, 5–6.

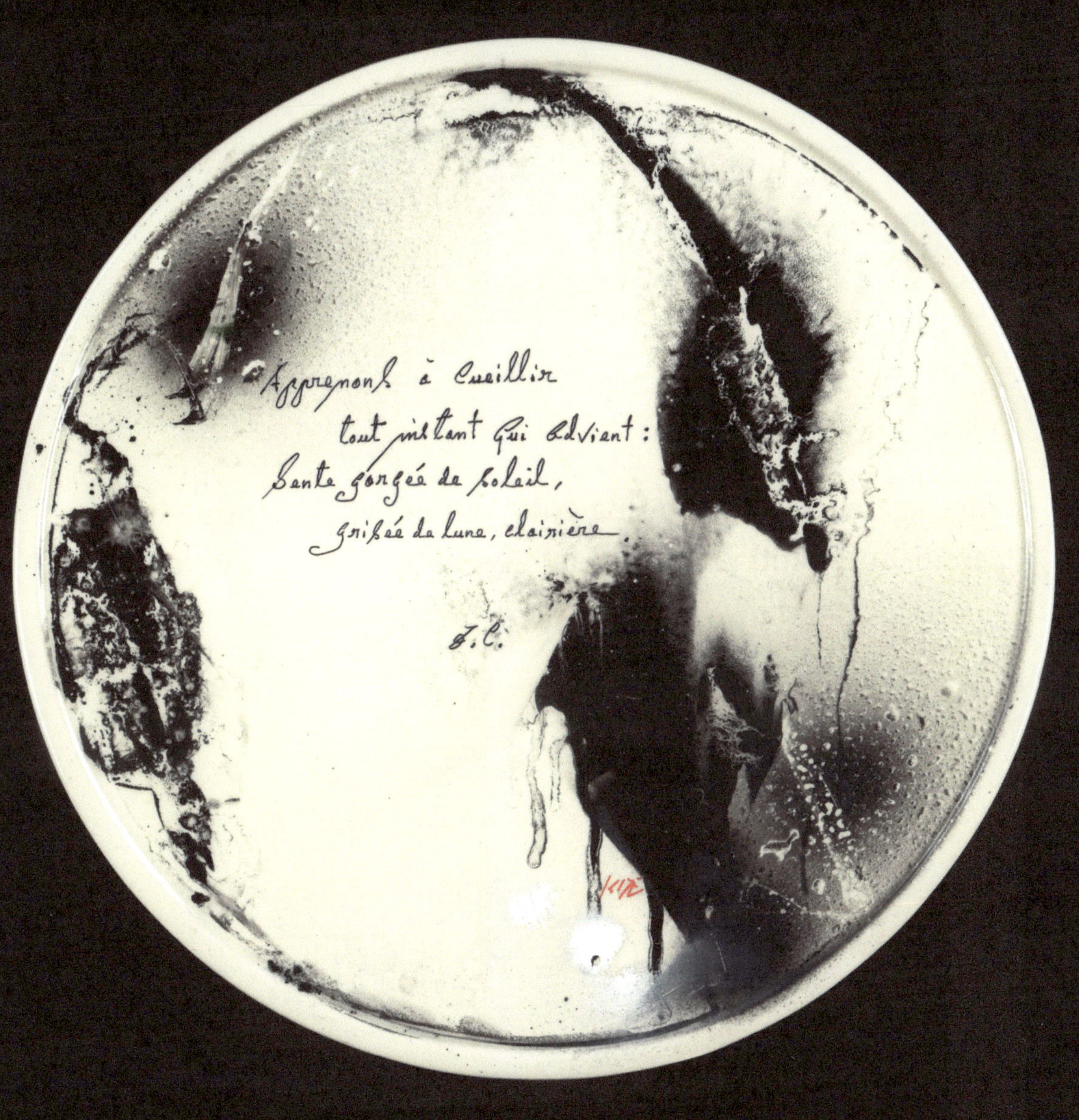
Apprenons à cueillir
tout instant qui advient :
sente gorgée de soleil,
grisée de lune, clairière.
J.C.

Once again, God is bringing good out of evil, accepting human foolishness and yet still somehow achieving . . . wise ends.[5]

5. *Sister Wendy's Bible Treasury*, 59.

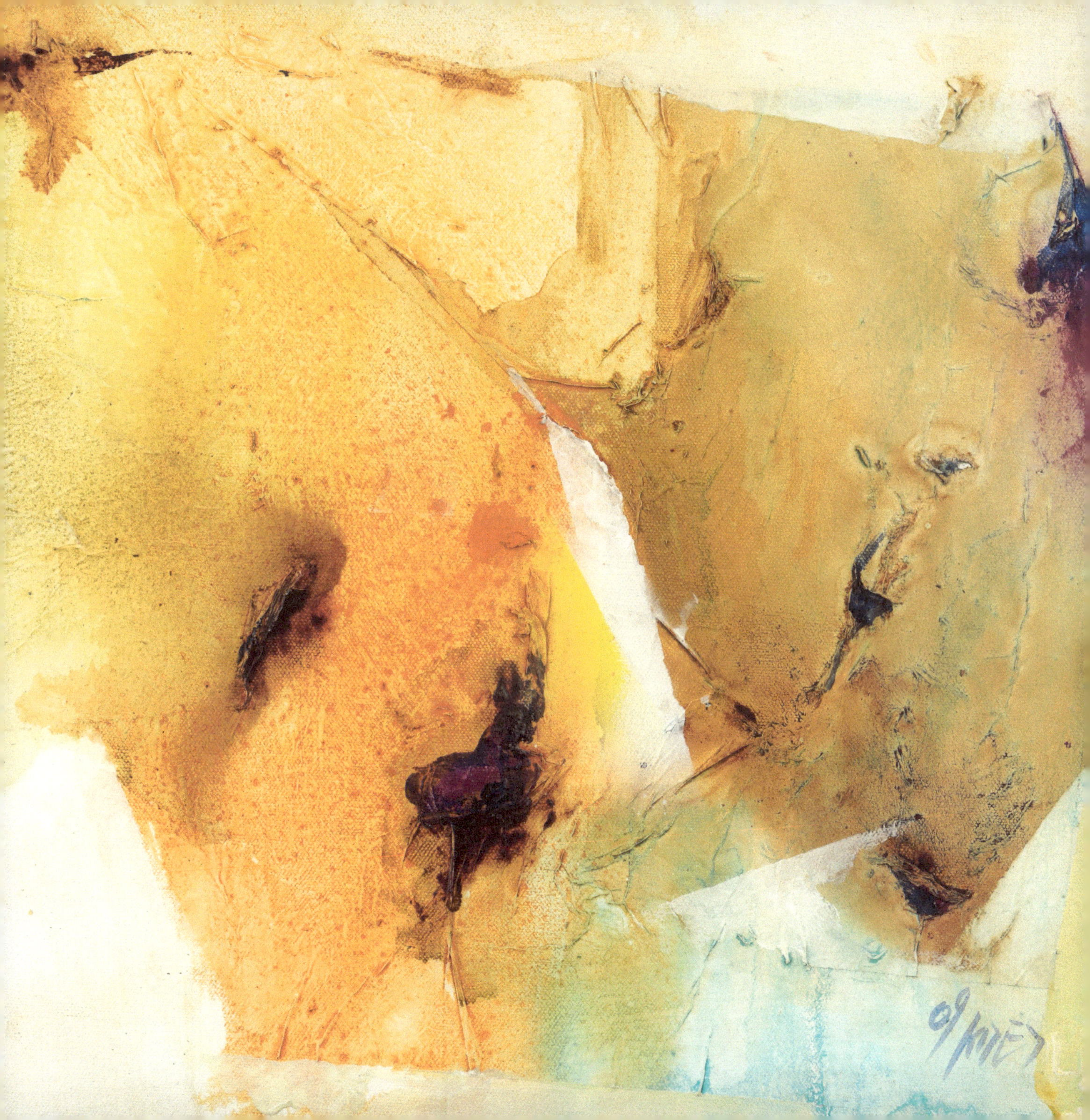

Prayer does not depend upon our natural capacity . . . Prayer itself is as simple as conversation between friends . . .[6]

6. *On Prayer*, 7.

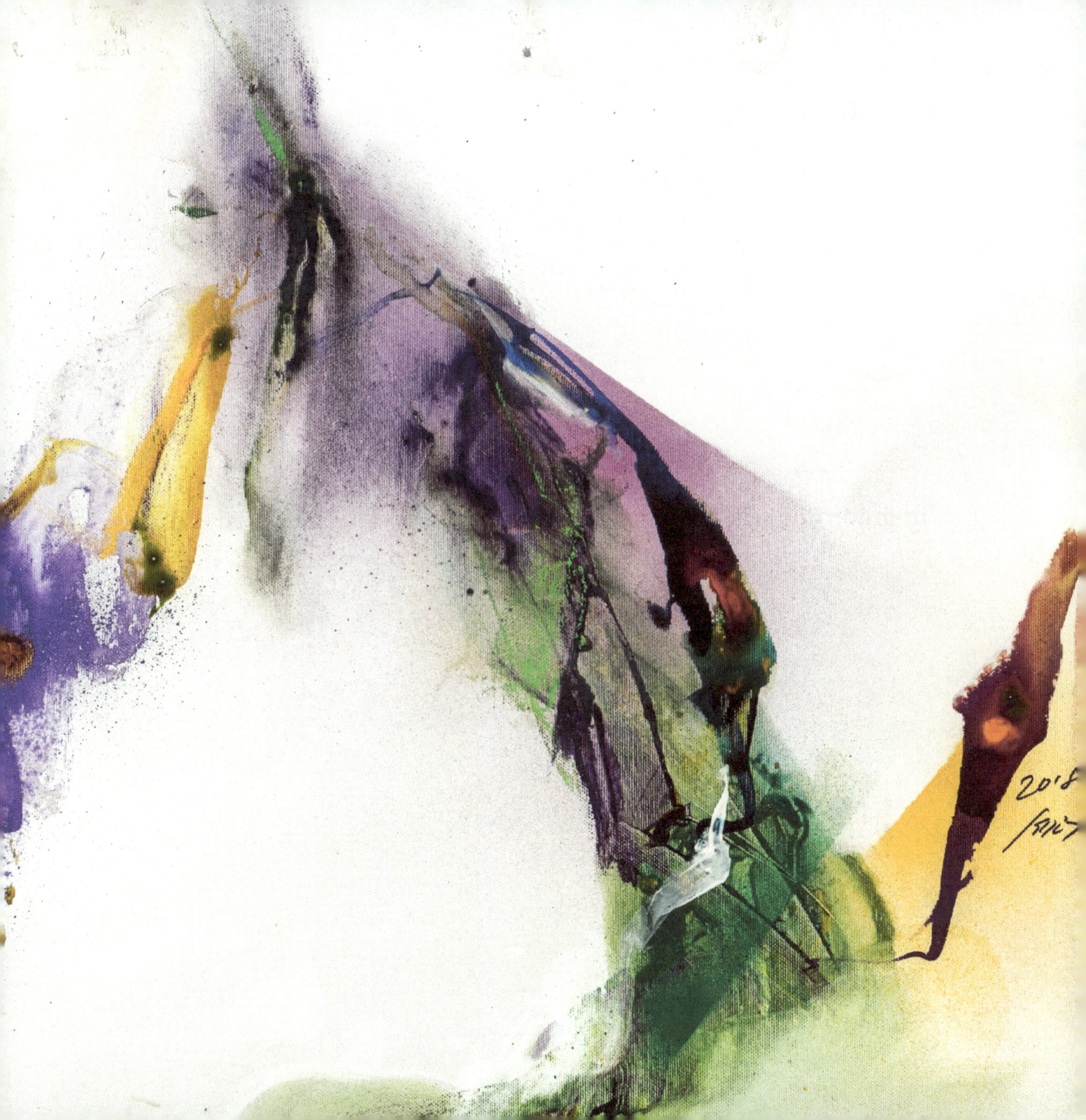
2018

In prayer the relationship is between God and ourselves. God is always the same, but each of us is completely different.[7]

7. *On Prayer*, 7.

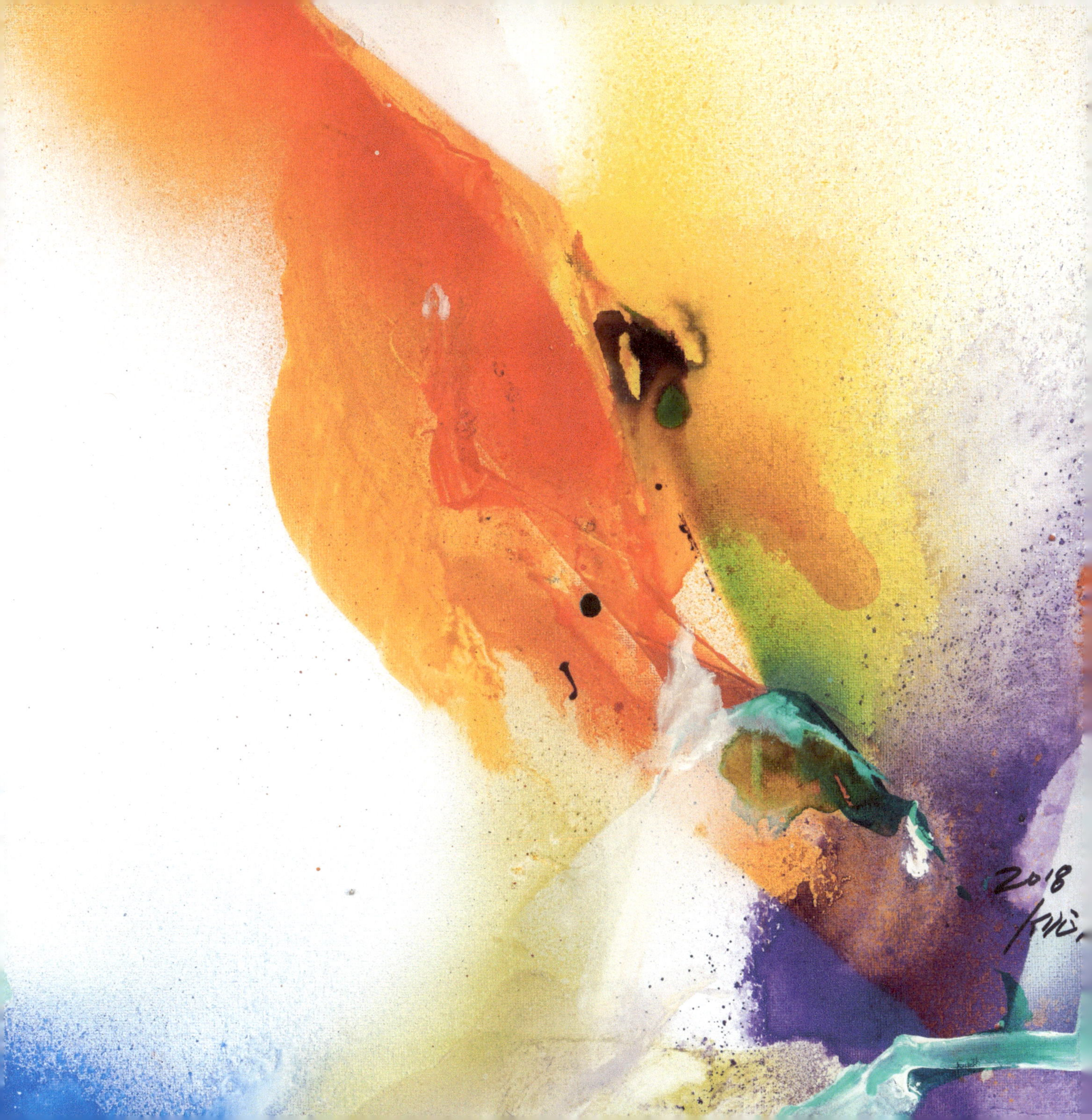
2018

The essential act of prayer is to stand unprotected before God . . .[8]

8. *On Prayer*, 8.

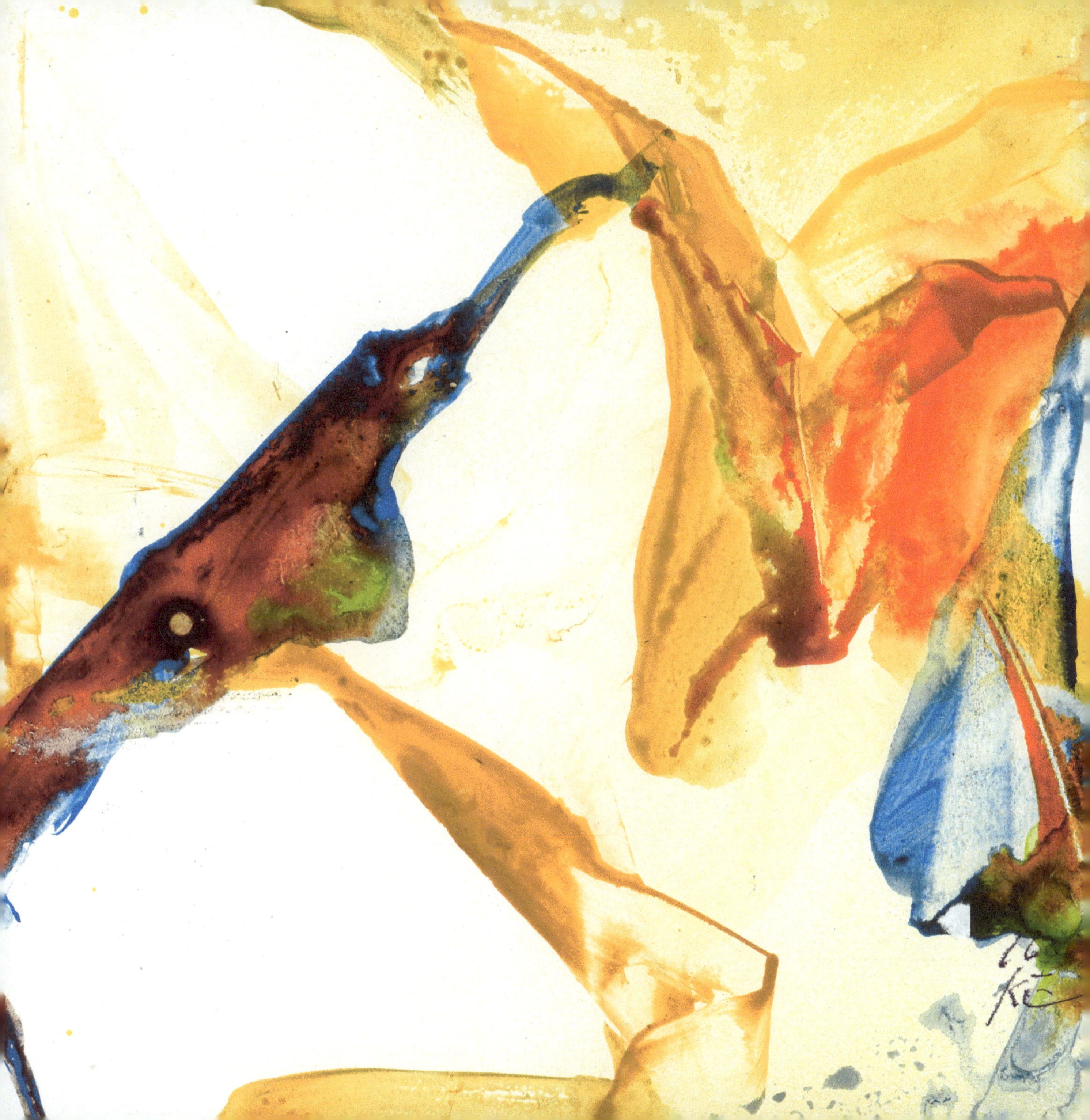

[Prayer] means having nothing left for ourselves, always bound to the will of Another, no sense of interior success to comfort us . . .[9]

9. *On Prayer*, 8.

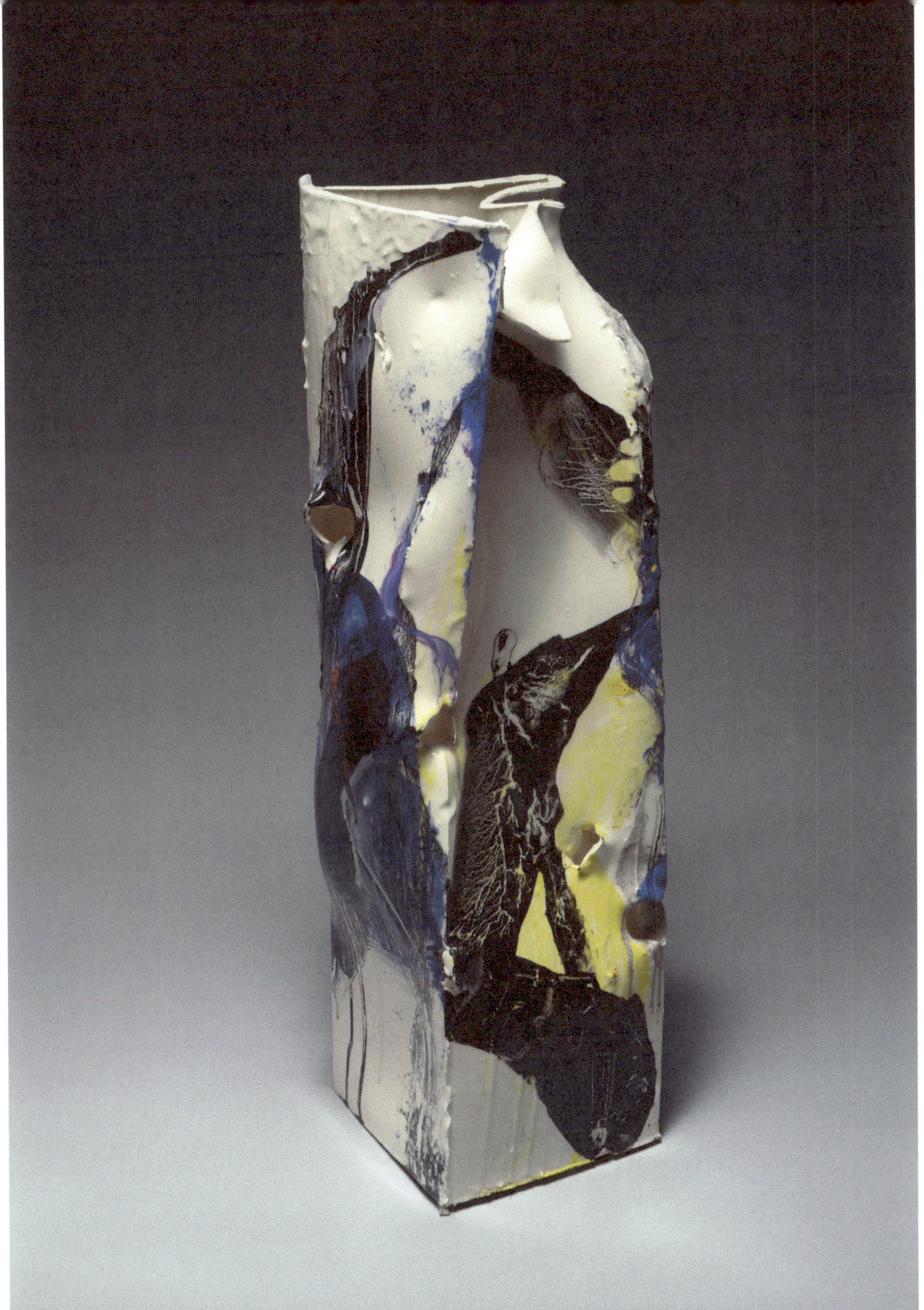

[Prayer means] living in the painful acknowledgment of being 'unprofitable servants'.[10]

10. *On Prayer*, 8.

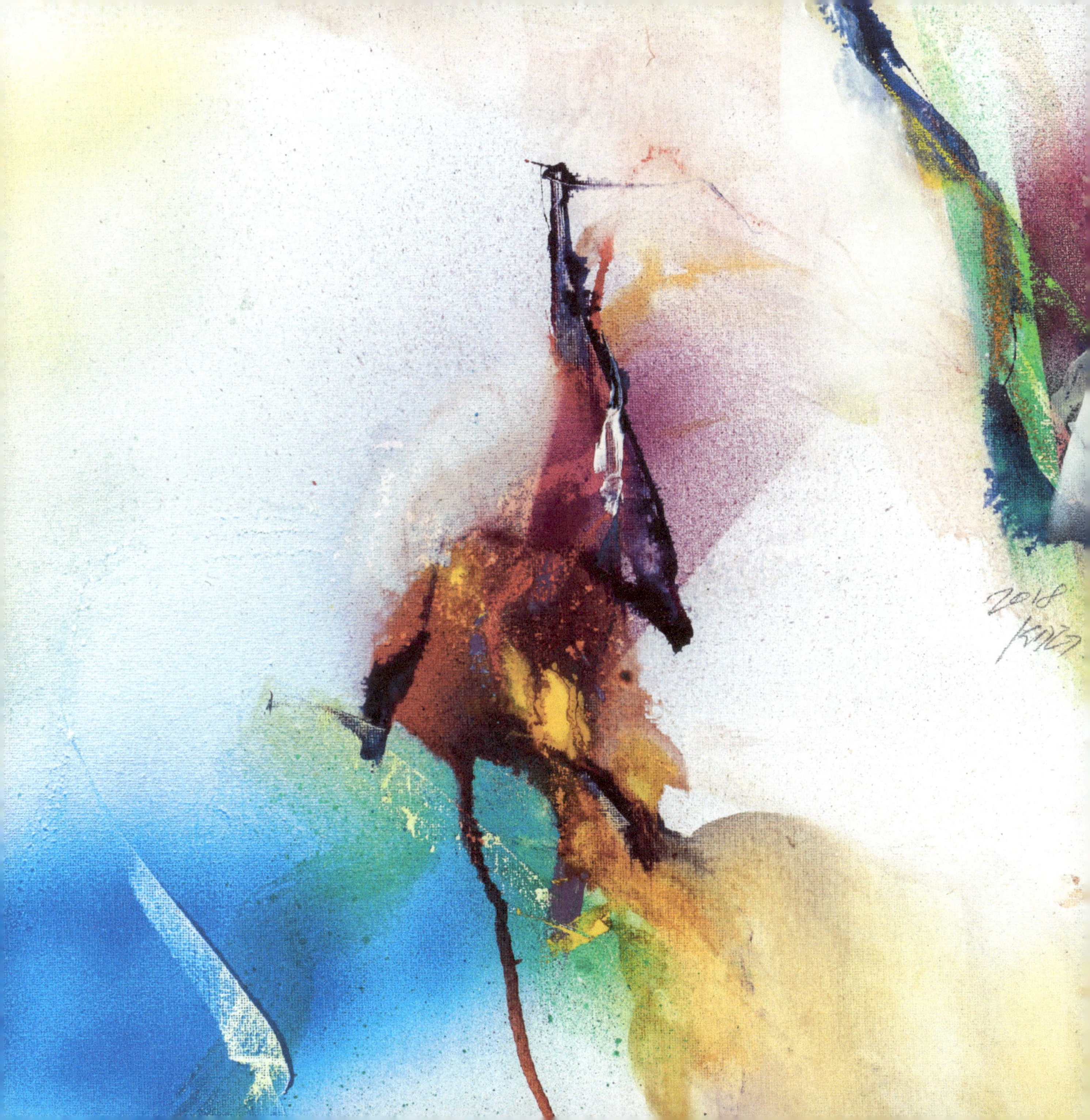
2018

. . . we need to keep our wits about us as we read these books of Scripture, and pay attention to not only to what they say, but also to what they intend.[11]

11. *Sister Wendy's Bible Treasury*, 118.

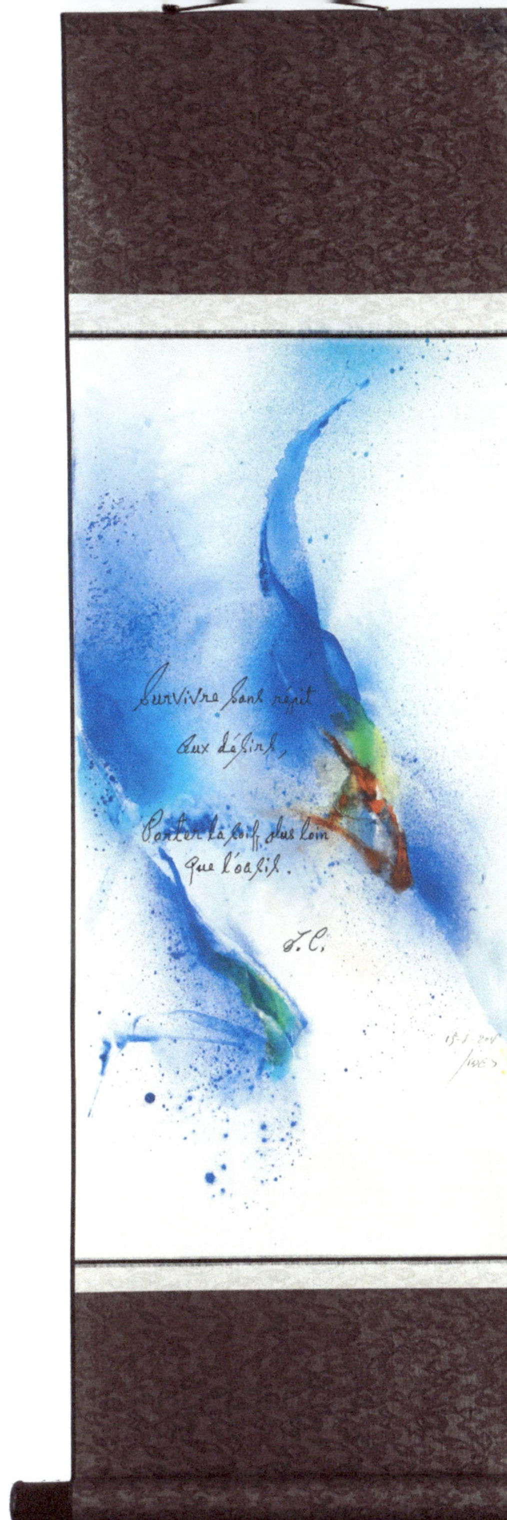
Survivre sans répit
aux désirs,
Porter la soif plus loin
que l'oasis.
J.C.

All revelation intends to open to us the secrets of God, but this opening may come in unexpected ways.[12]

12. *Sister Wendy's Bible Treasury*, 118.

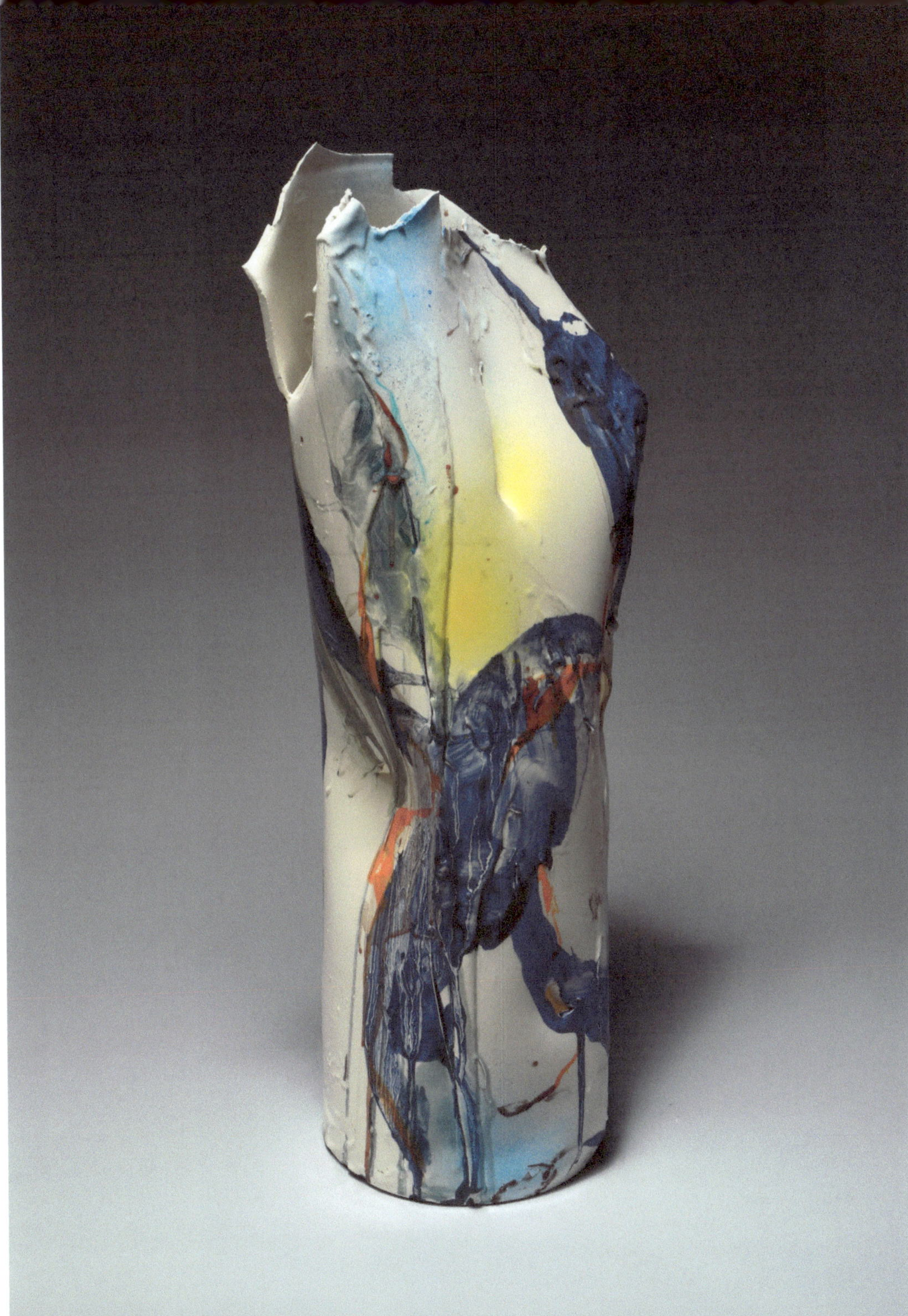

In silent prayer there are no words and hence no thoughts.[13]

13. *On Prayer*, 16–17.

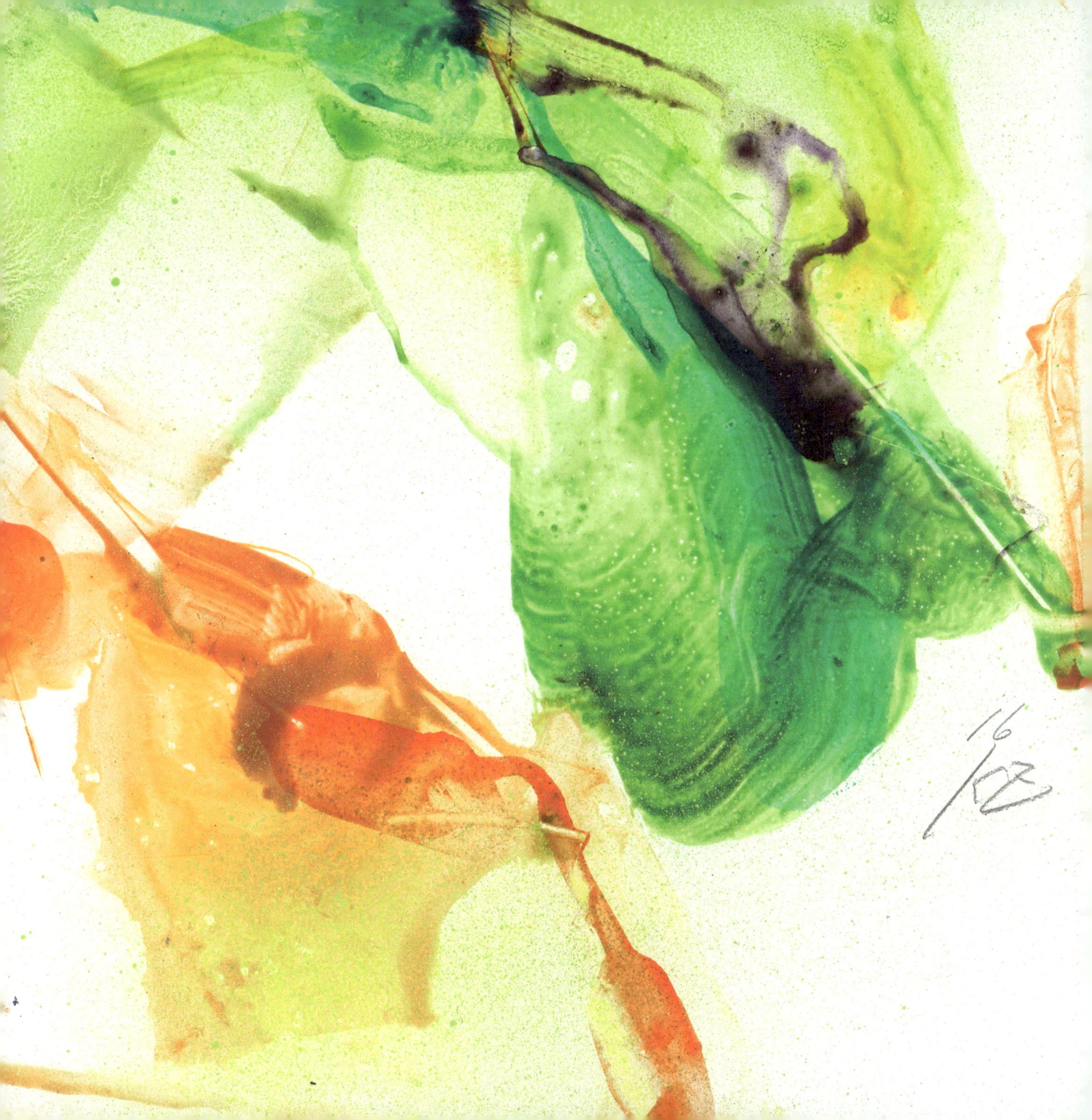

[In silent prayer] We are still. This silence is nothing to be afraid of.[14]

14. *On Prayer*, 16–17.

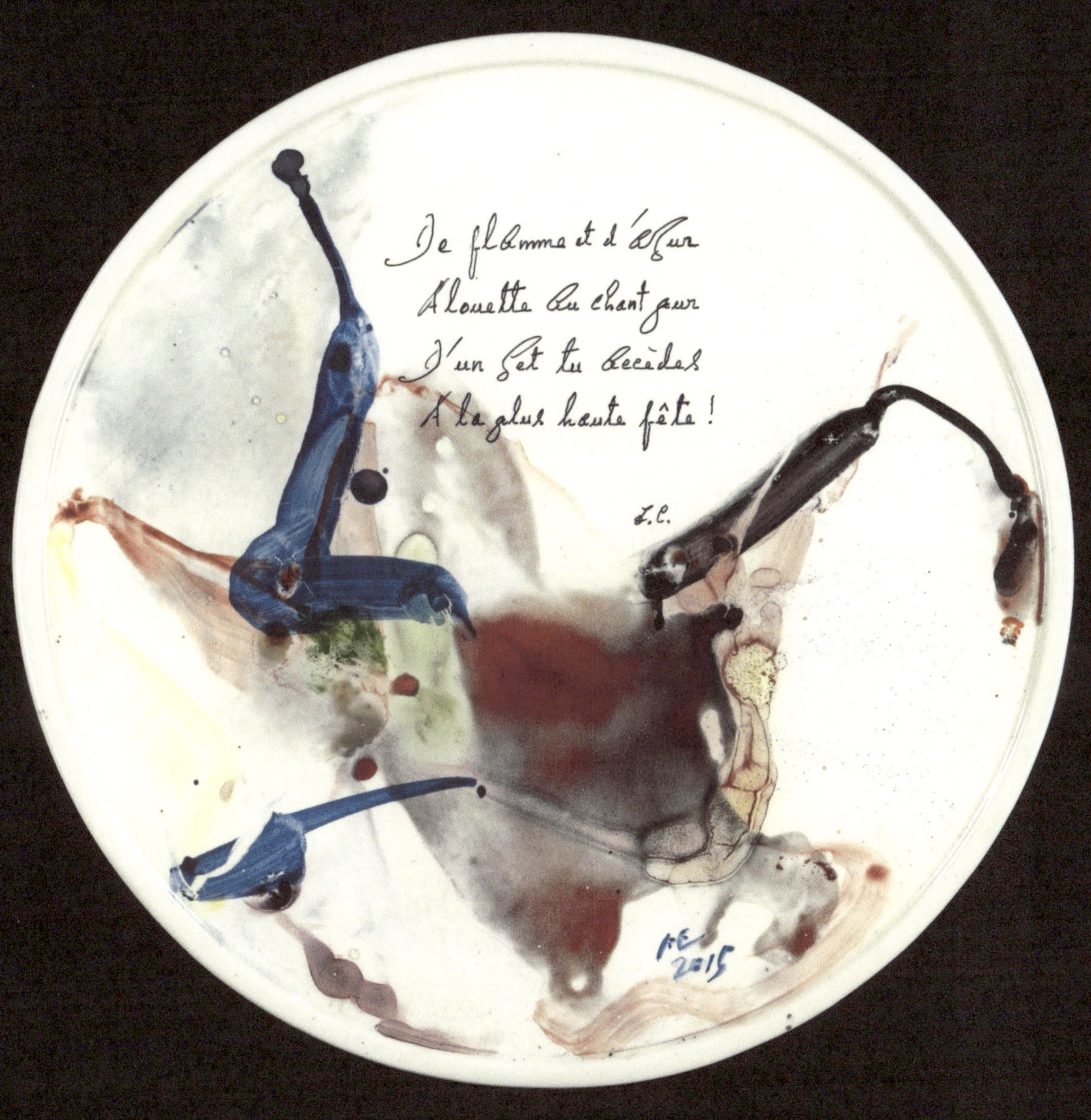

De flamme et d'azur
Alouette au chant pur
D'un jet tu accèdes
À la plus haute fête !
F.C.
FE 2015

This is how we want God's people to move towards their destiny [that is] with love and dignity and consideration of others . . . it may be that there is not much of it in ordinary life. But it does exist to comfort and inspire us . . . [15]

15. *Sister Wendy's Bible Treasury*, 65.

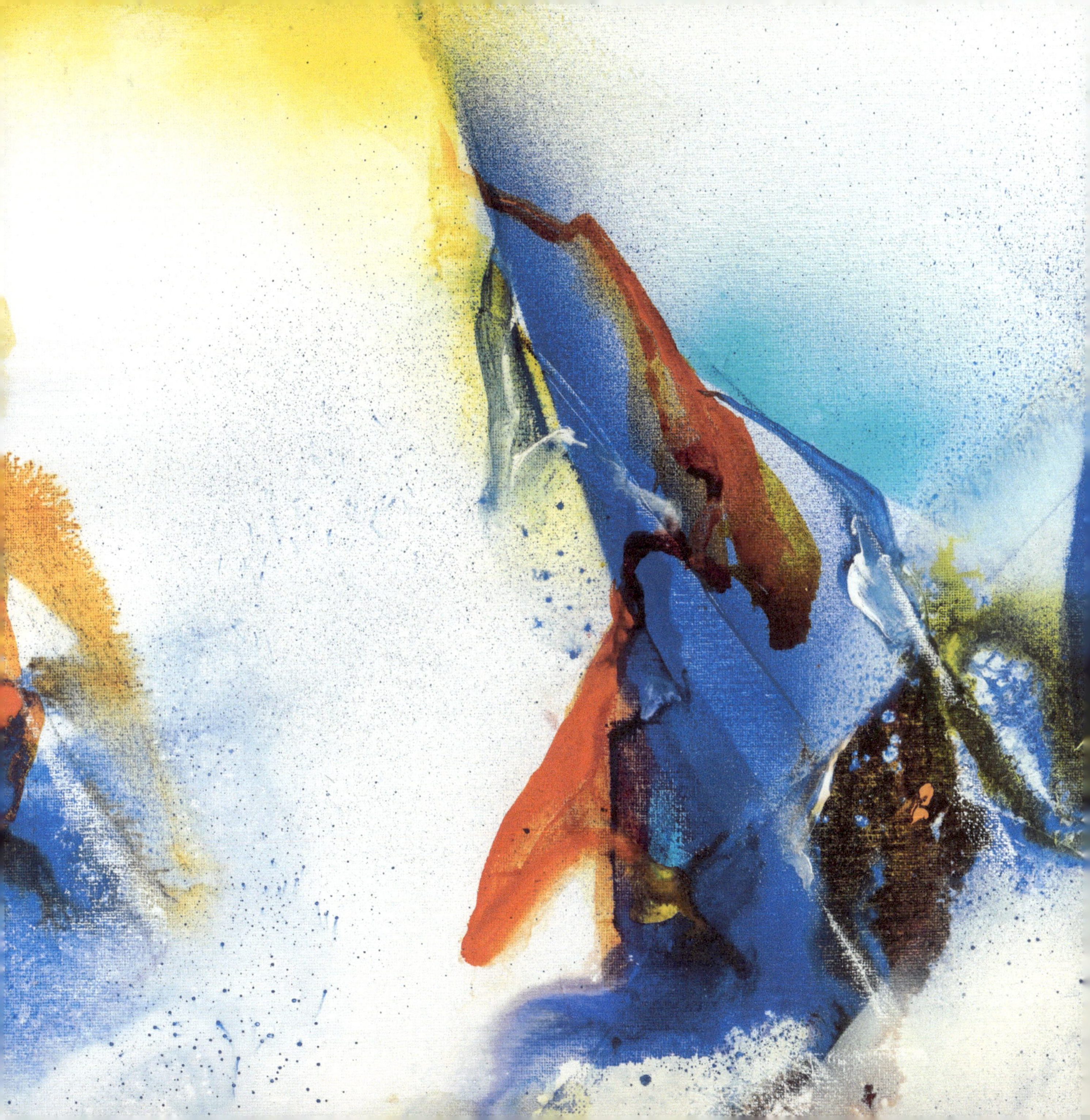

All religions are based on prayer, on a true, living contact with the living God.[16]

16. *On Prayer*, 54.

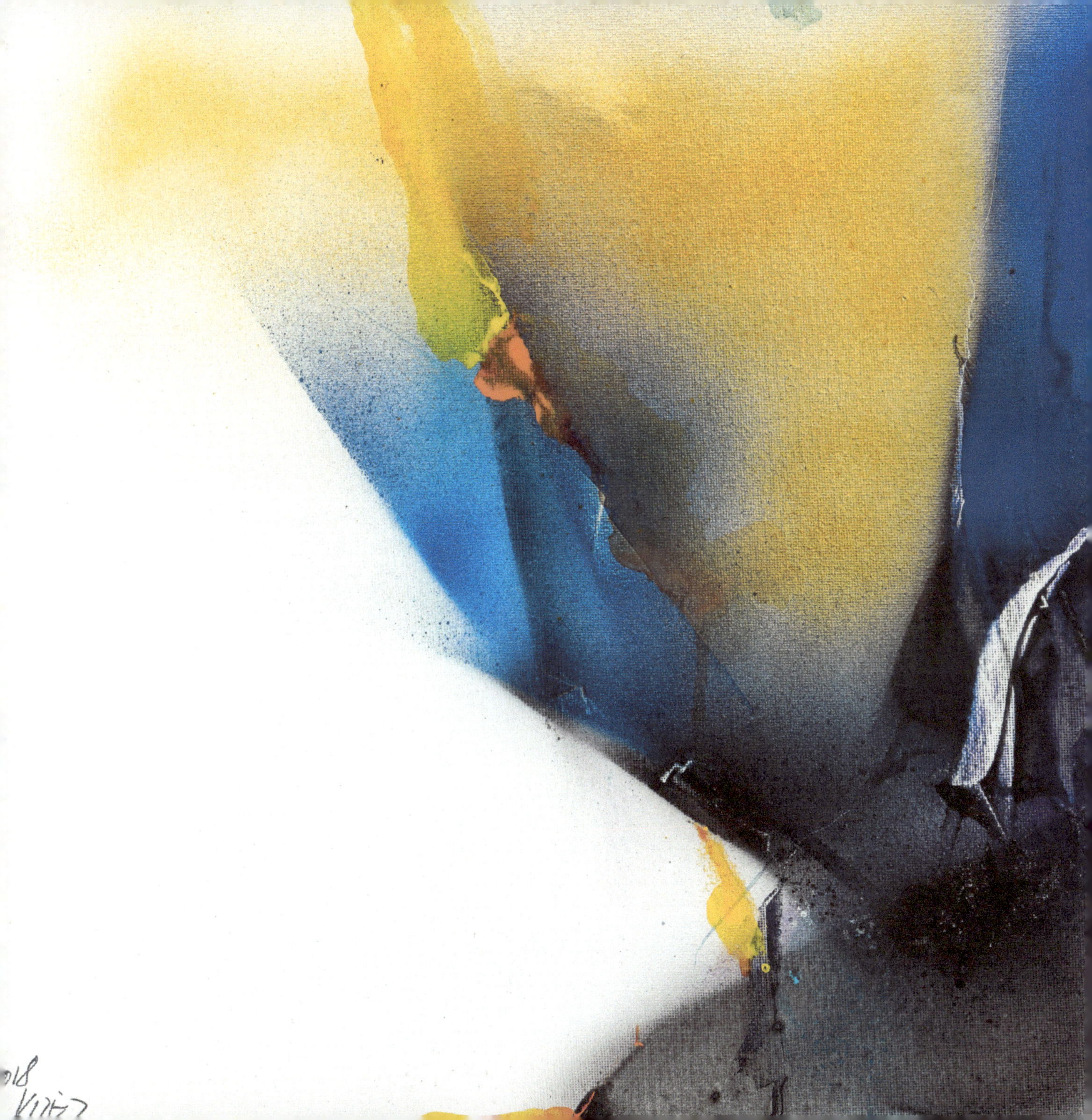

Whatever your religion, if you pray, you want to be taken up into God and used for the world.[17]

17. *On Prayer*, 55.

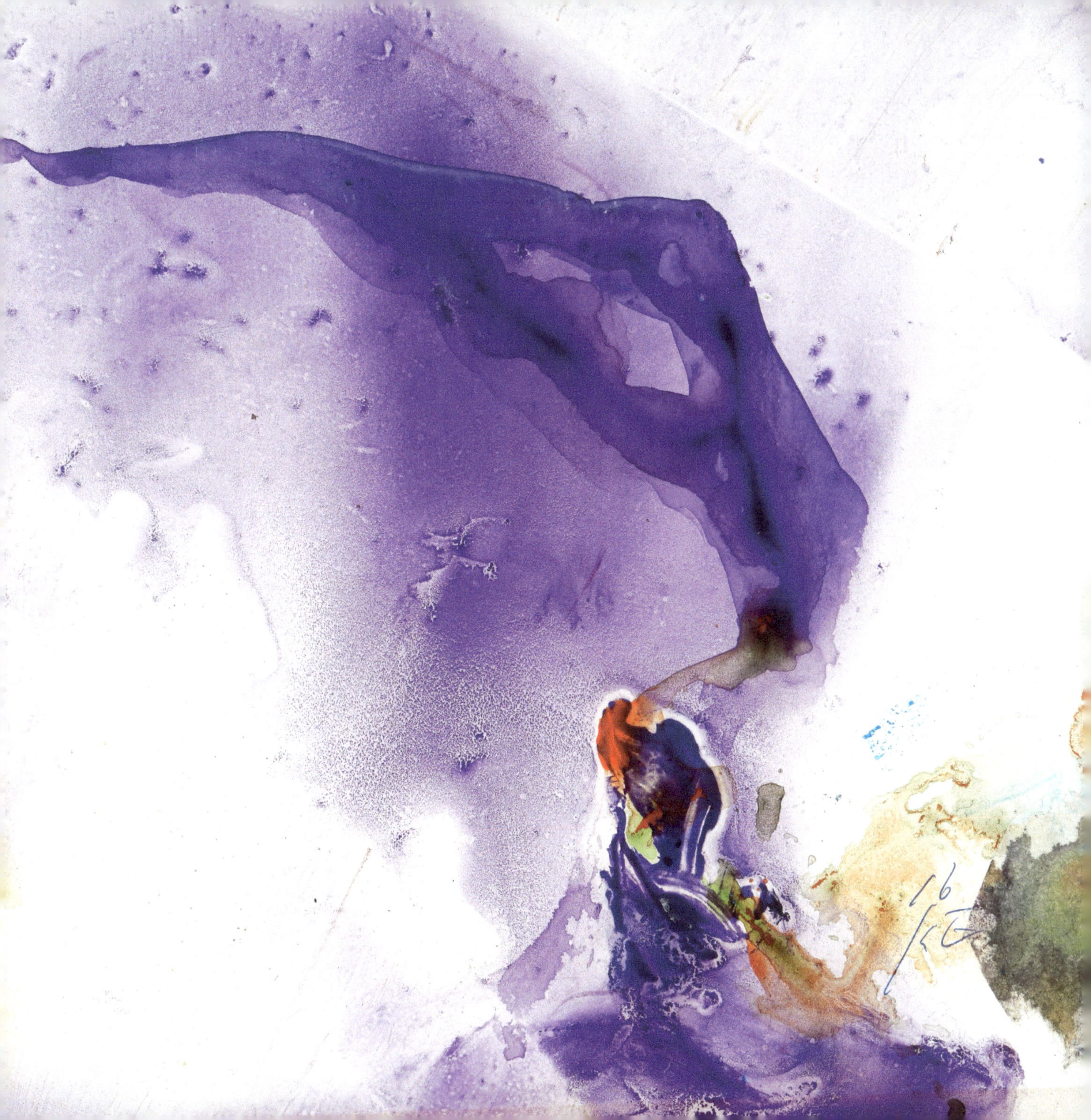

No gift from God is just for ourselves. It is always for using, for other people. [18]

18. *On Prayer*, 55.

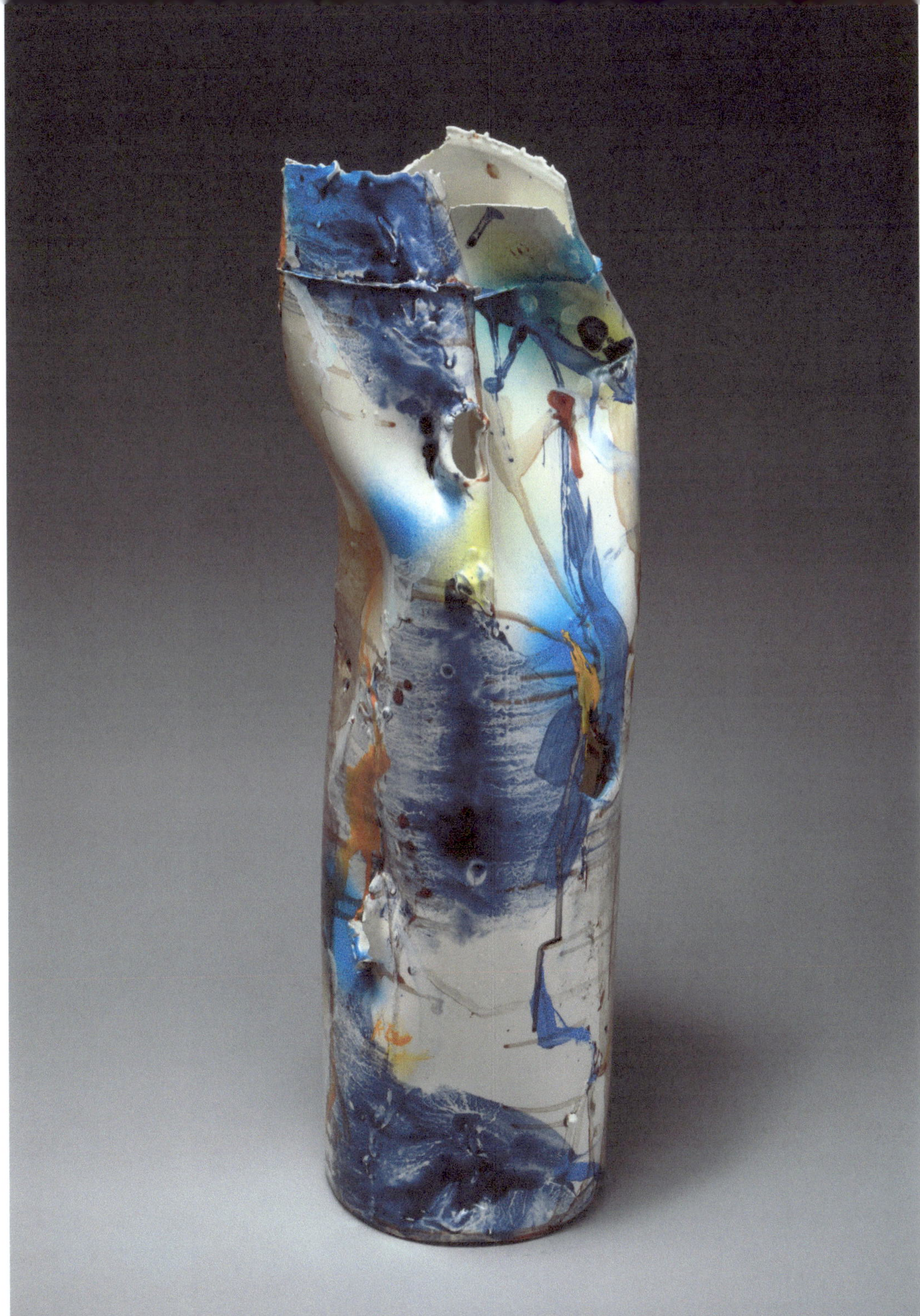

A prophet is not one who foresees the future . . . rather [is] one who explains the significance of the present. Yet that present is pregnant with the future . . .[19]

19. *Sister Wendy's Bible Treasury*, 126.

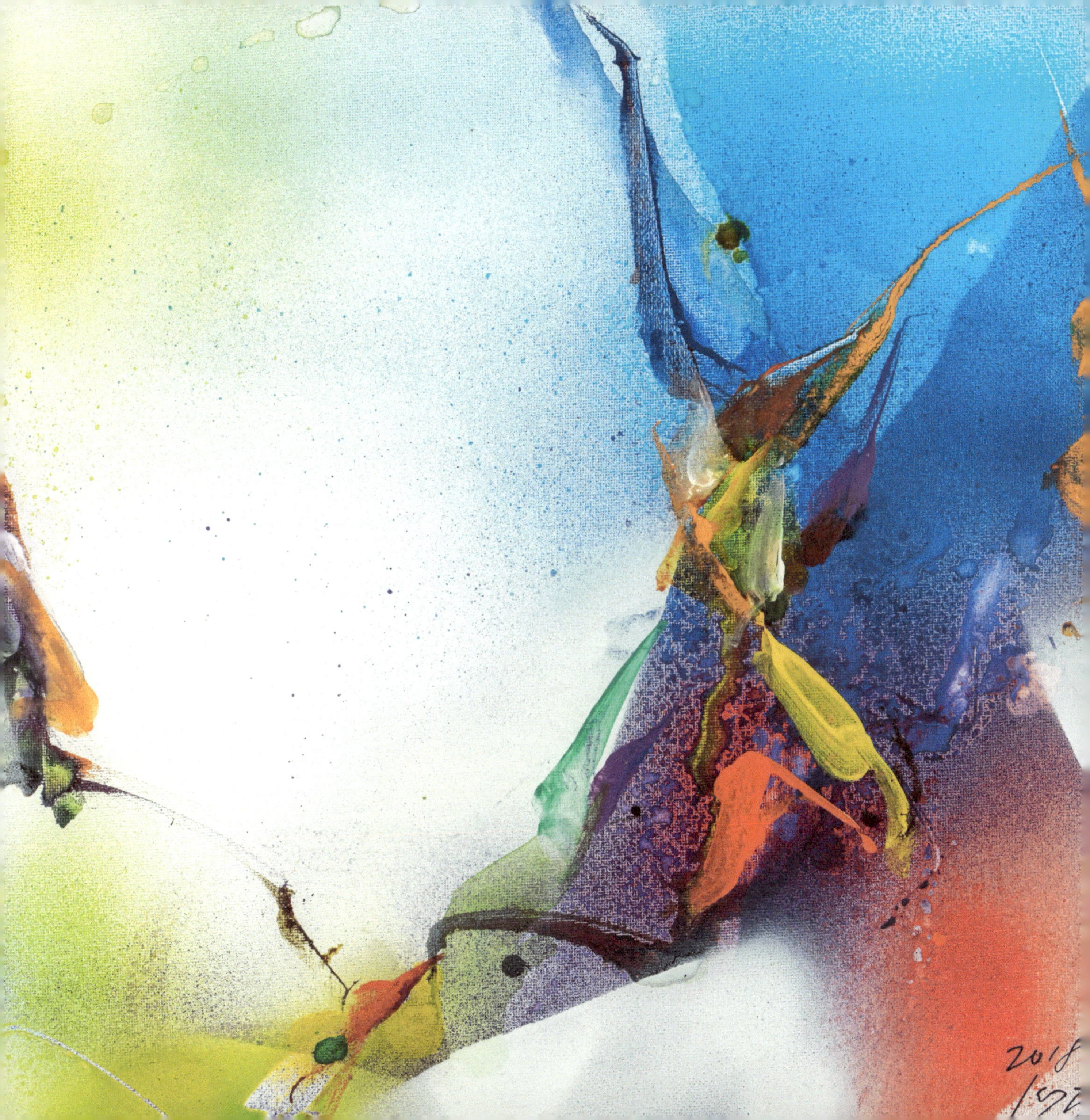
2018

Prayer has to do with God, ever present, ever loving, and with you yourself, as present and receptive of God's love as you are able.[20]

---

20. *On Prayer*, 76.

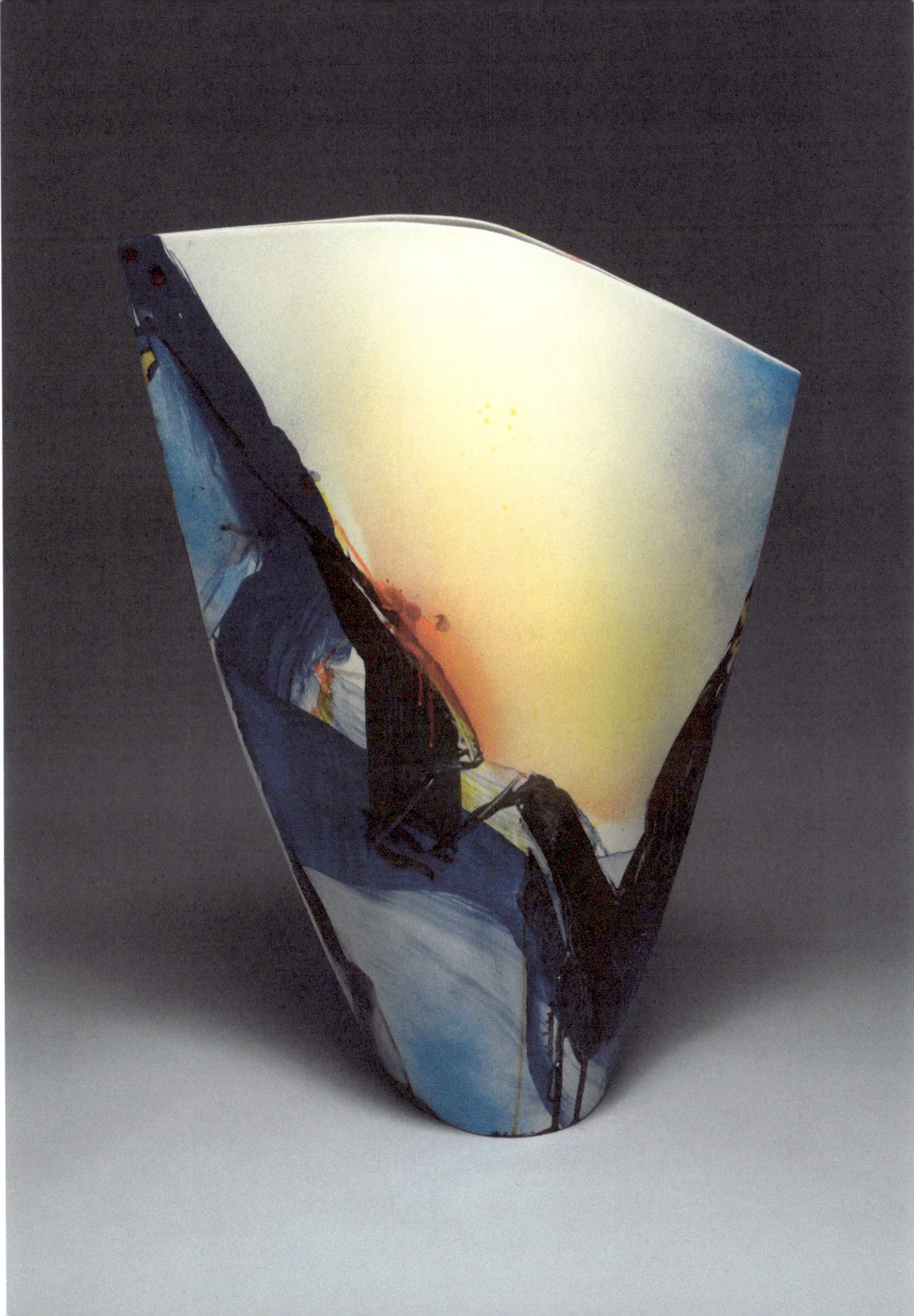

Matisse, in a pure, true world of his own, a world of vision.[21]

21. *Spiritual Letters*, 199.

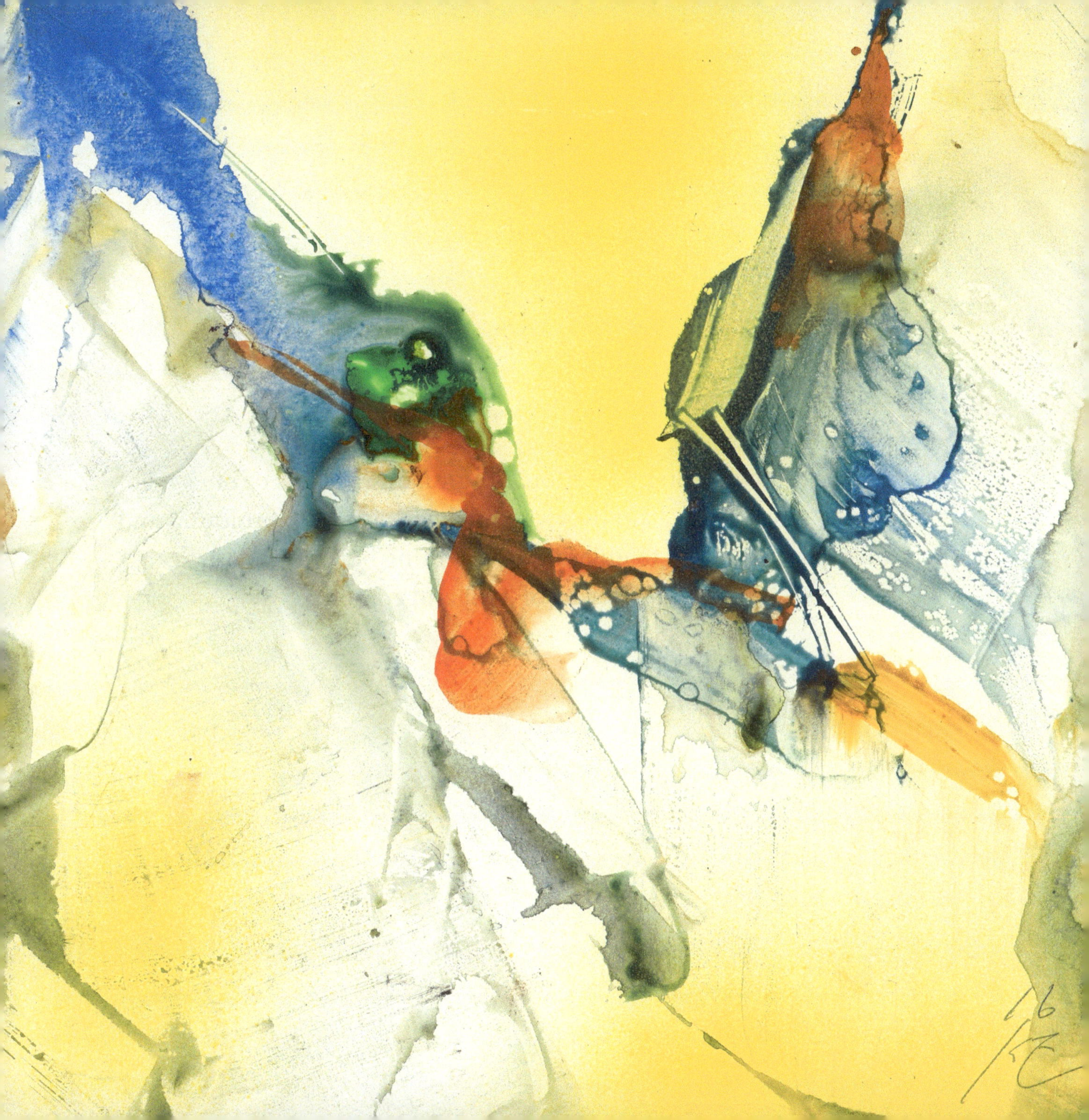

Art . . . A drawing on into a more profound awareness of one's own unique humanity . . . I am overwhelmed with joy . . . a profound and transforming joy, a call to enter into something beyond what is seen . . . expressed in terms of light and colour . . . [22]

22. *On Prayer*, 77.

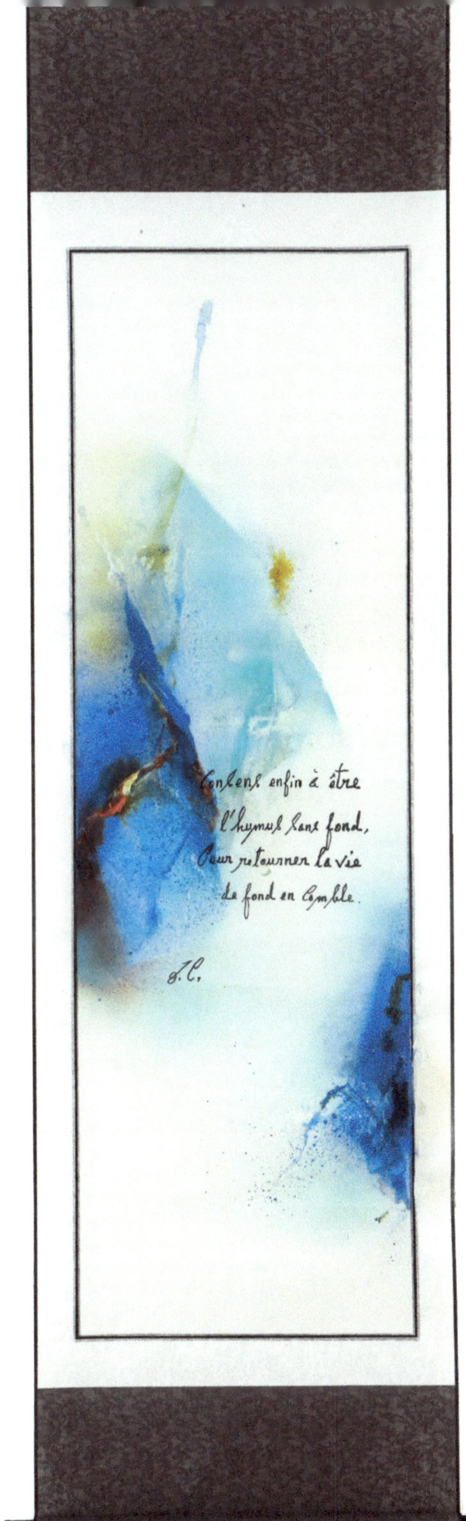
Consens enfin à être
l'humus sans fond,
Pour retourner la vie
de fond en comble.

[With art] I know that I have been lifted out of my smallness and into something immeasurably great, something that, however vaguely, seems 'holy'.[23]

23. *On Prayer*, 77.

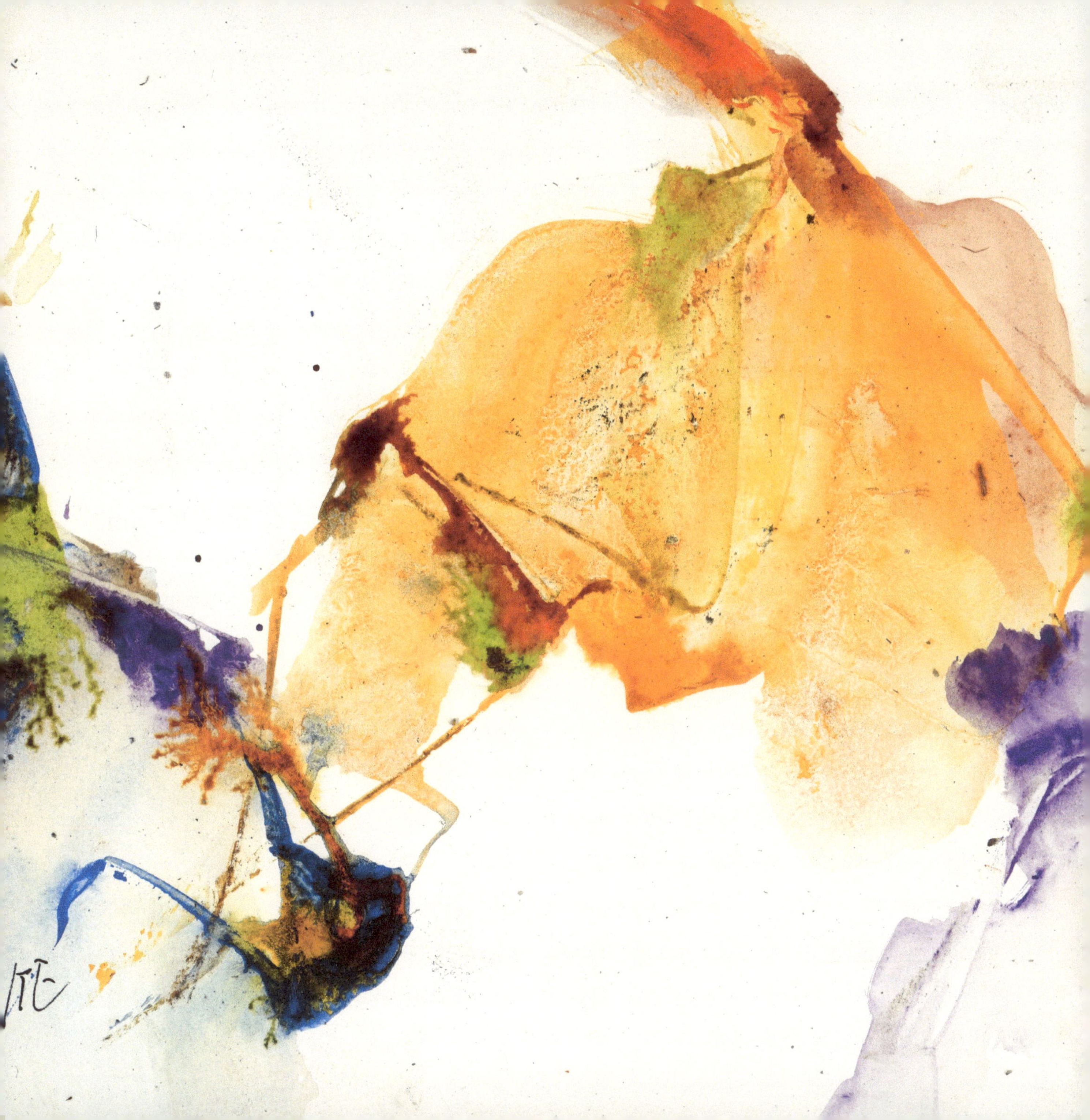

I cannot even think of writing about myself. I cannot 'see' myself. I am lost in the overpowering Reality of God.[24]

24. *Spiritual Letters*, 291.

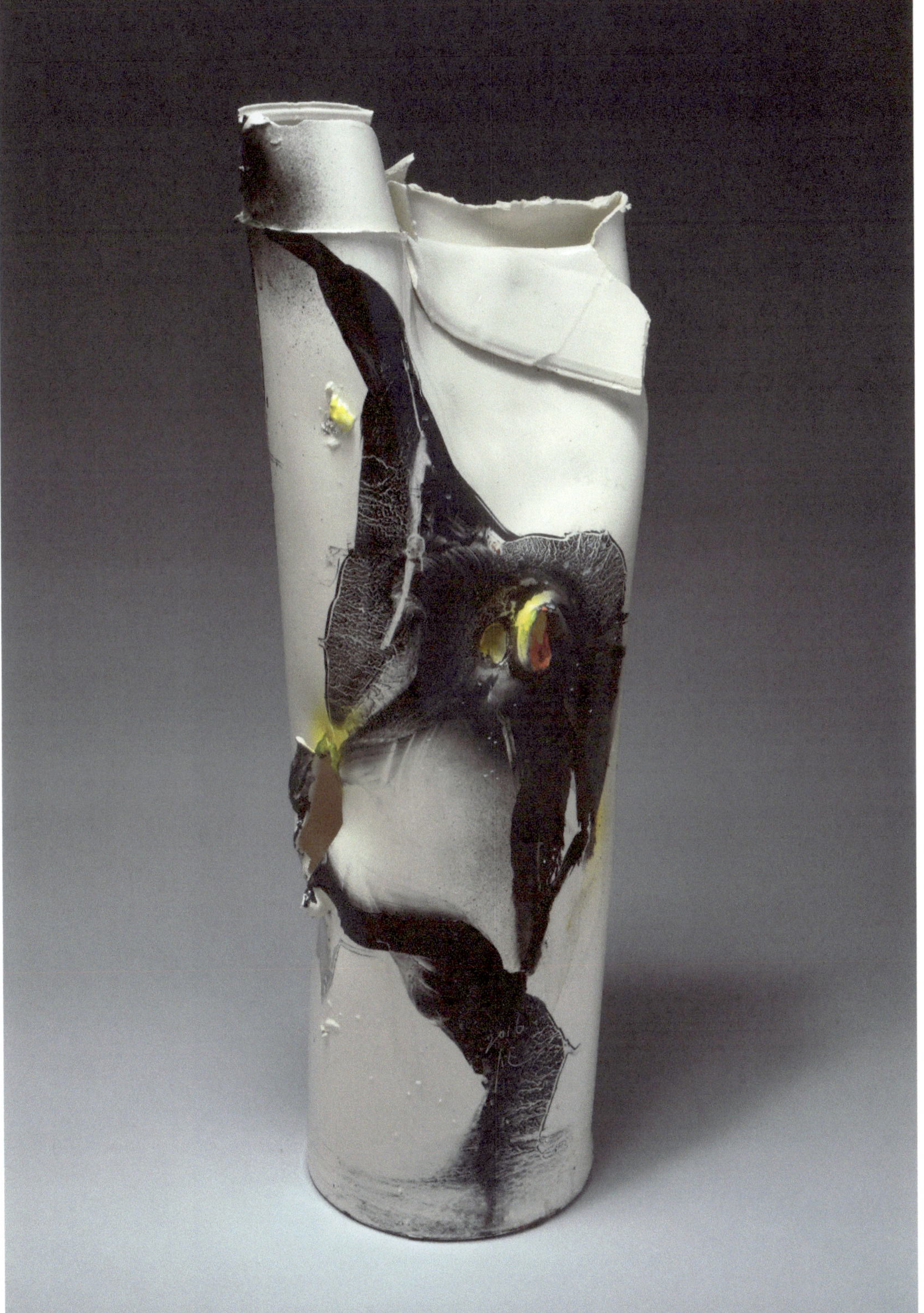
2016

Whenever we speak about prayer, we are really speaking about the power of the Holy Spirit. We are not conscious of this all-powerful Spirit, nor can we be . . . [who] eludes all our perceptions.[25]

25. *On Prayer*, 90.

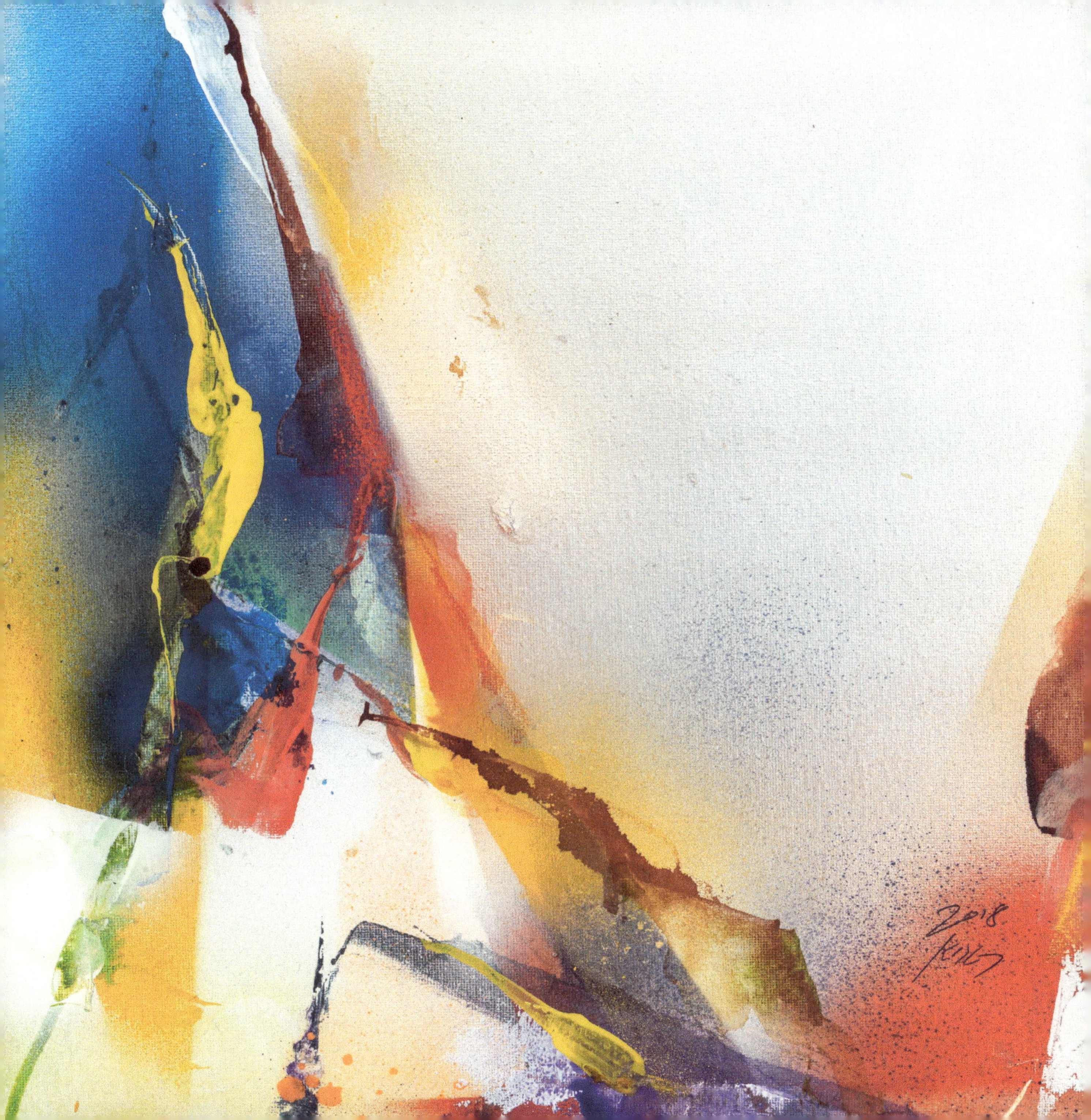

[in prayer] . . . our trust, which means love-in-action, comes into full play.[26]

26. *Spiritual Letters*, 286.

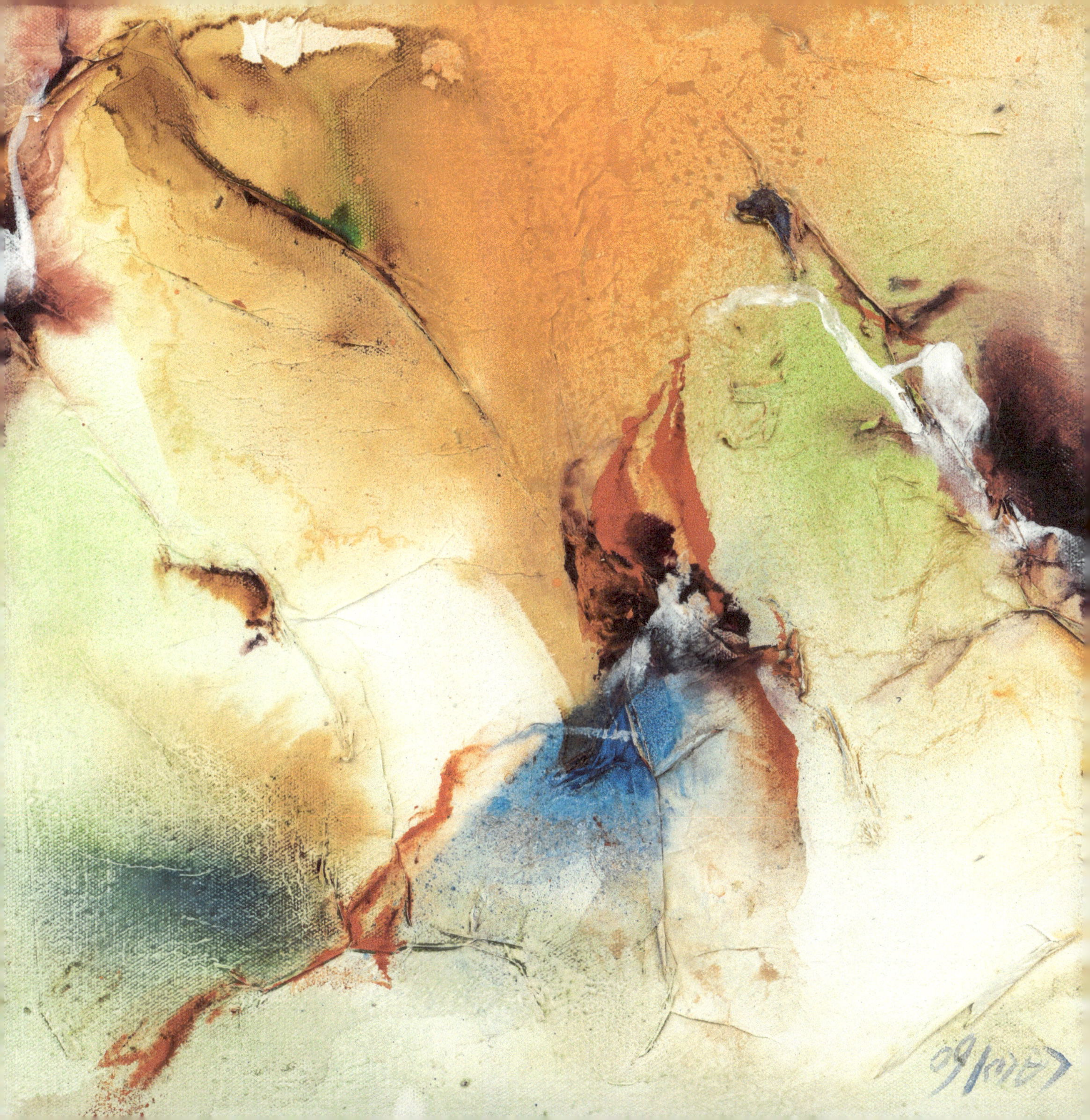

In prayer . . . God comes very close to us, but . . . does not speak in words.[27]

27. *Sister Wendy's Bible Treasury*, x.

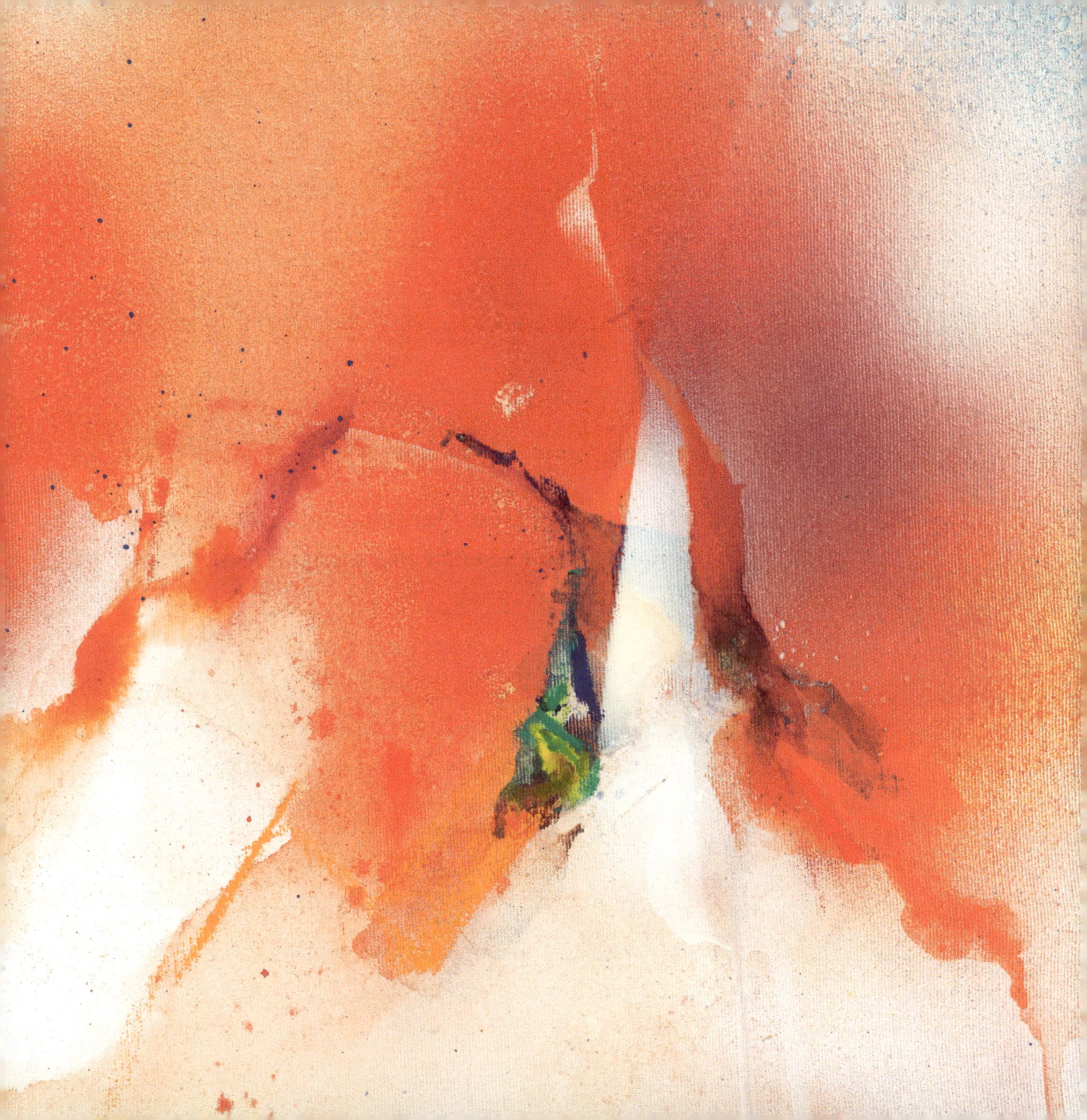

. . . no artist can truly picture God. Our imaginations cannot comprehend [God], no concept can encompass [God].[28]

28. *Sister Wendy's Bible Treasury*, 4.

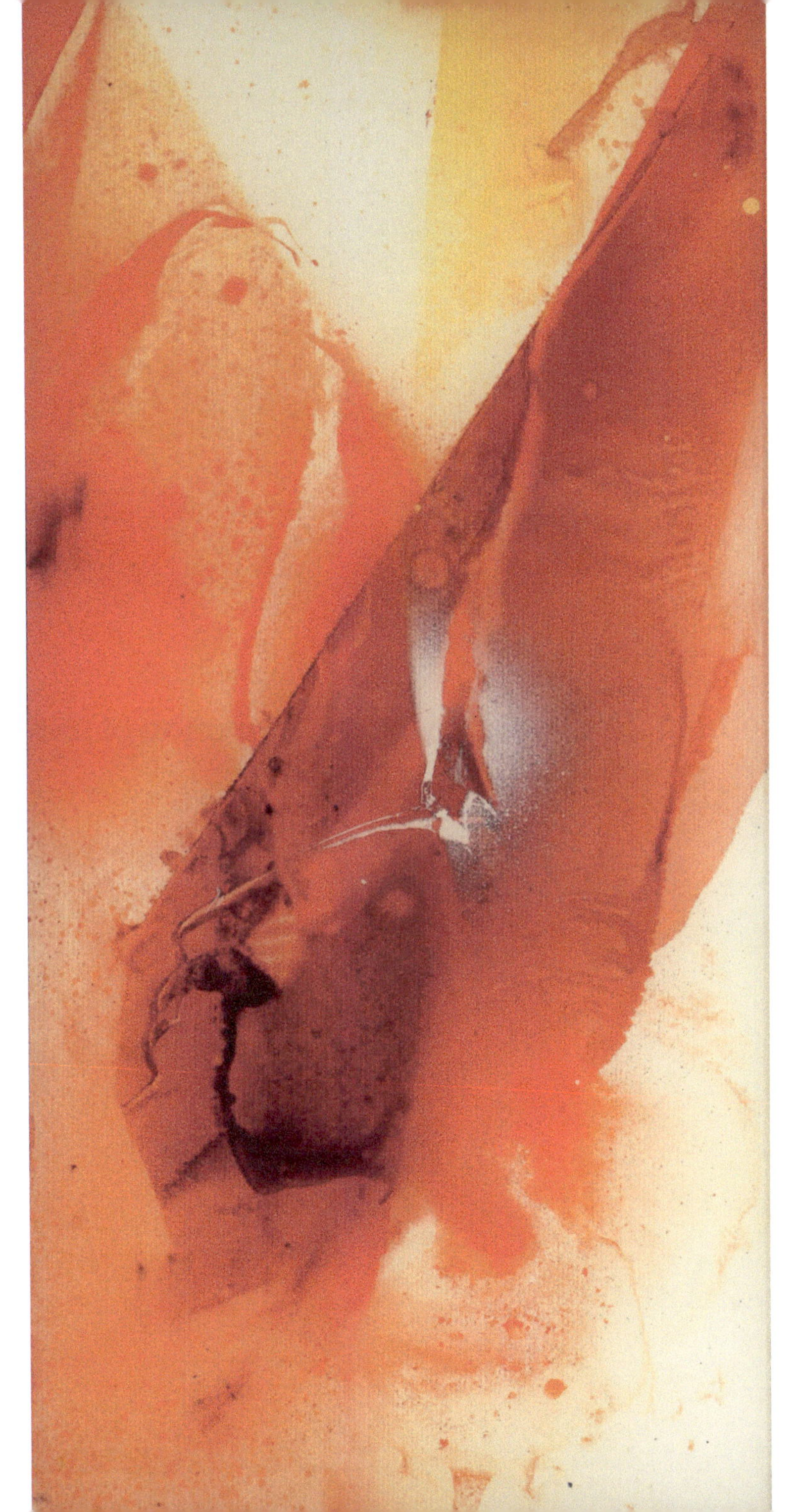

Humility is nothing to do with having a low opinion of our qualities . . .[29]

29. *On Prayer*, 91.

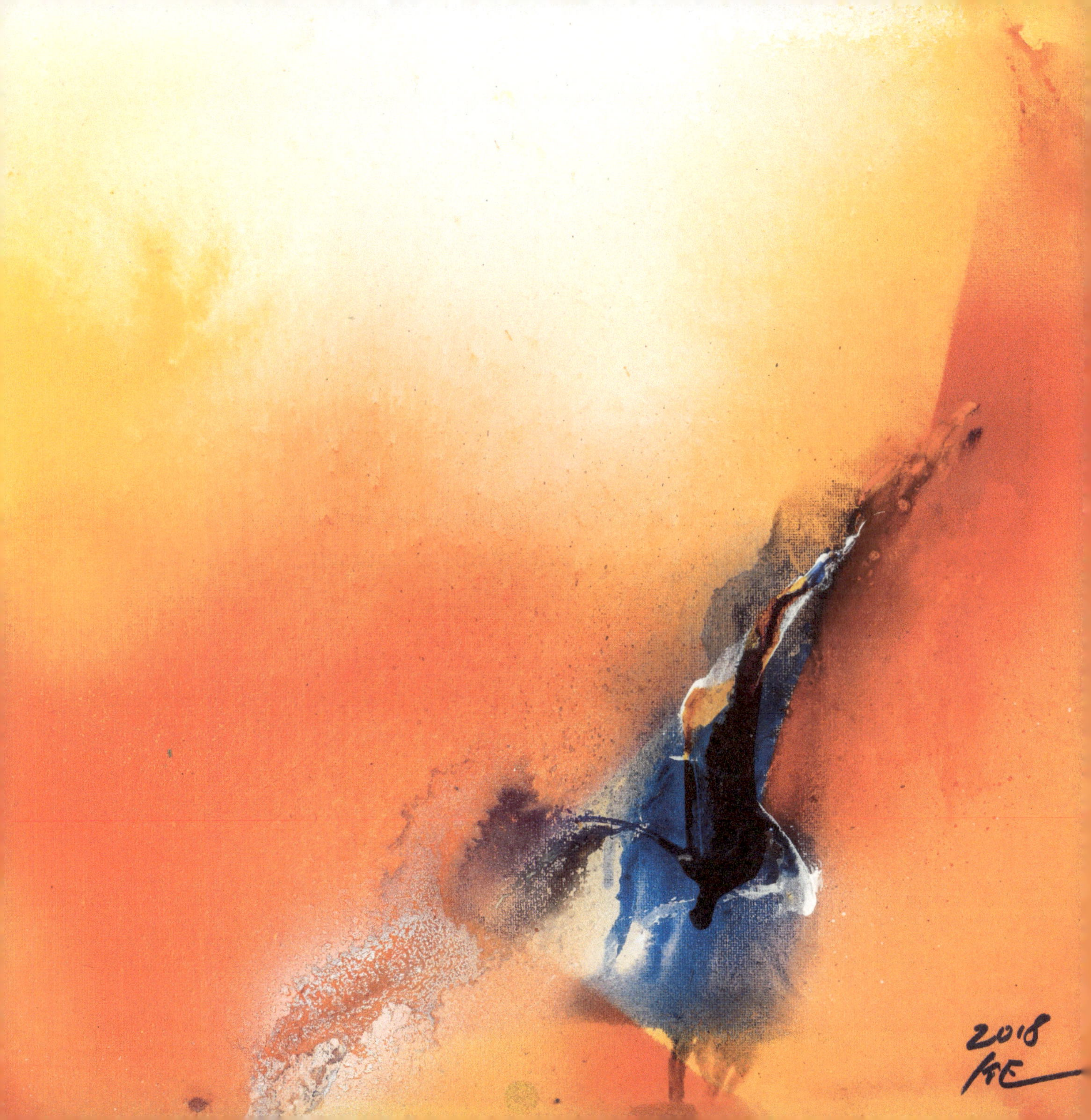
2018

[Humility] it is all to do with being interested in [our qualities], not gazing long and devotedly at yourself.[30]

30. *On Prayer*, 91.

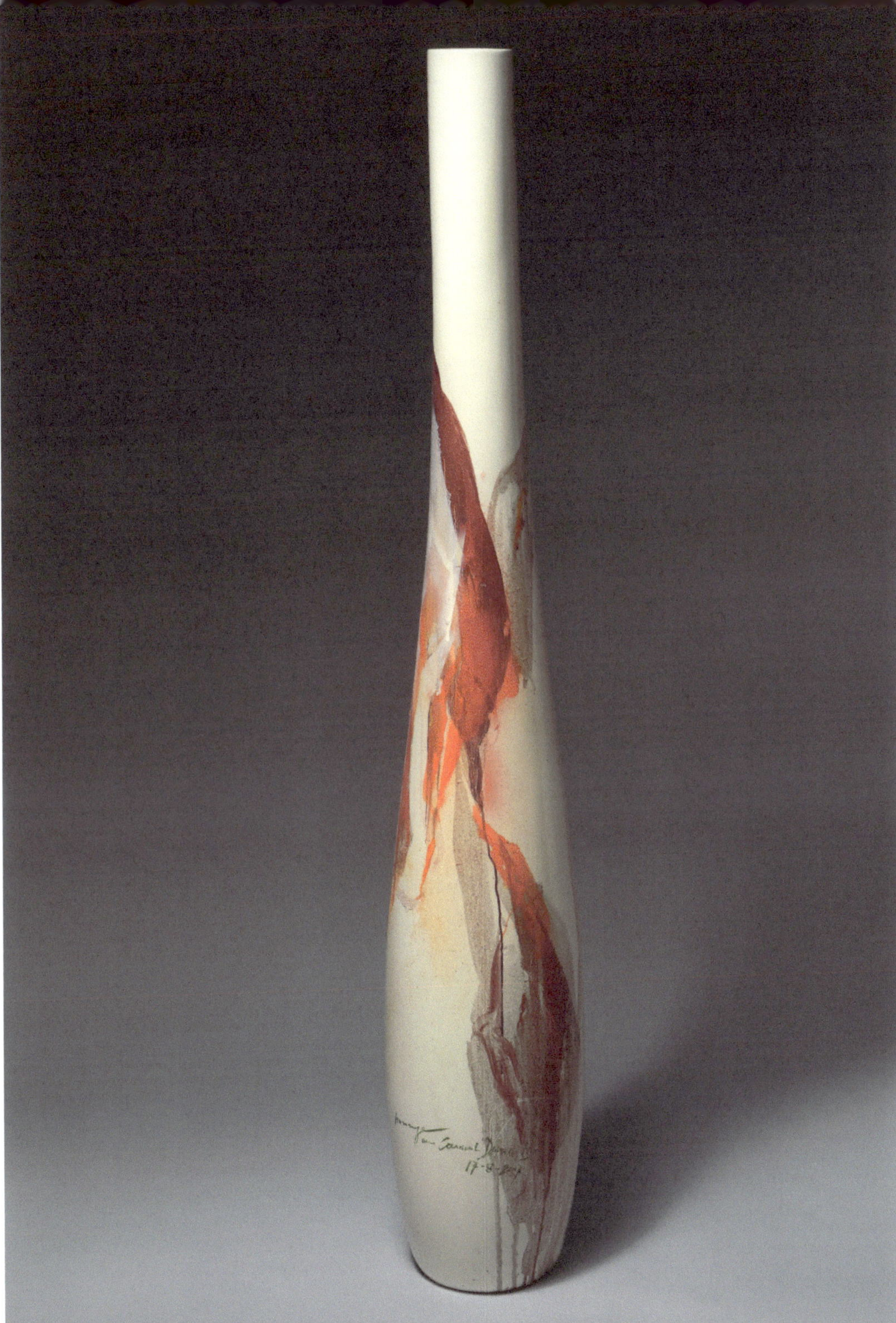

All that God gives us in prayer is not just for ourselves, but for others.[31]

31. *On Prayer*, 92.

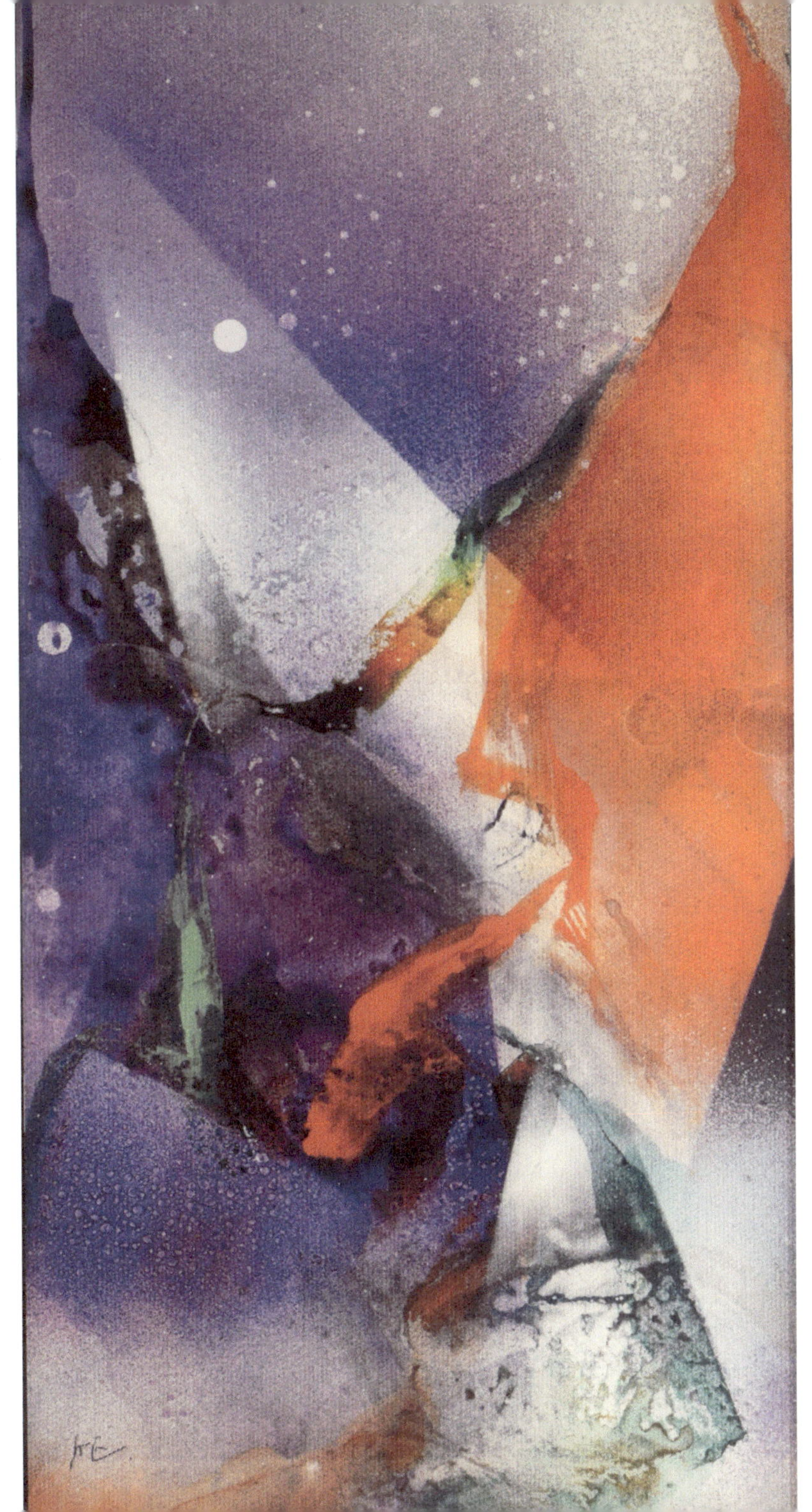

We can hear God's word in the strictly spiritual passages of the Bible. But one of its most important messages is that [God] also speaks through material and secular events.[32]

32. *Sister Wendy's Bible Treasury*, x.

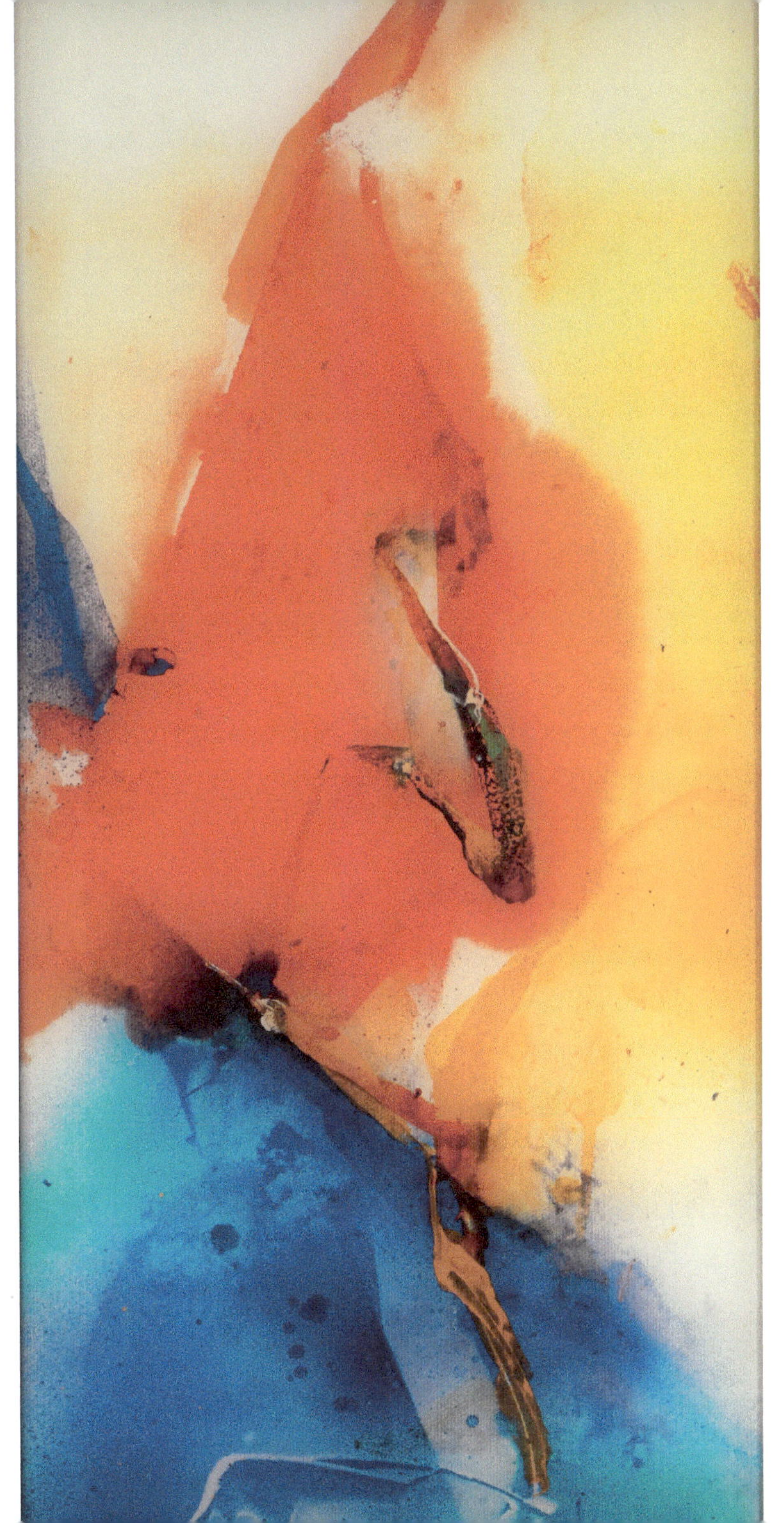

God works through all human activity.[33]

33. *Sister Wendy's Bible Treasury*, 13.

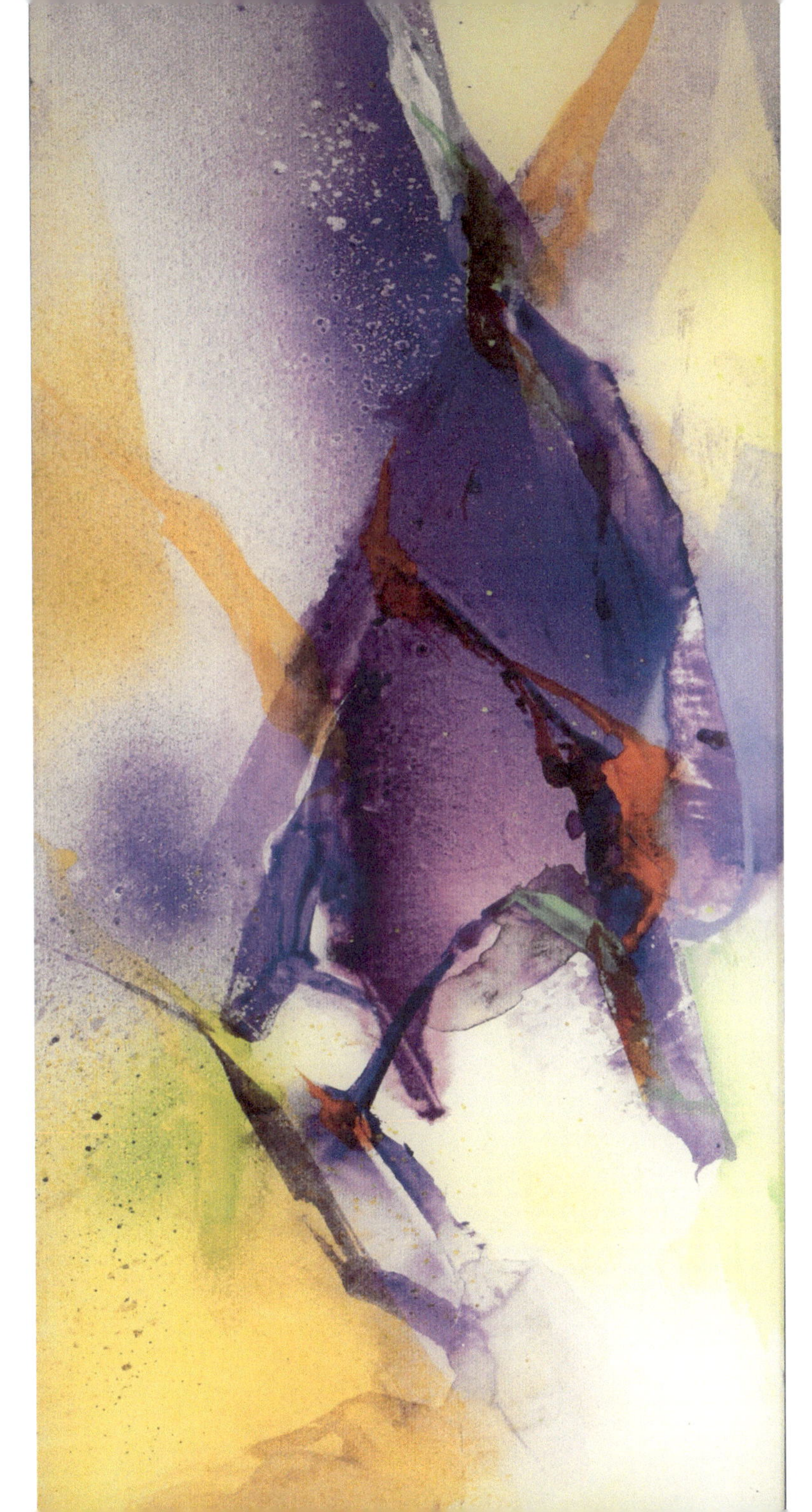

Love always seeks knowledge.[34]

34. *On Prayer*, 121.

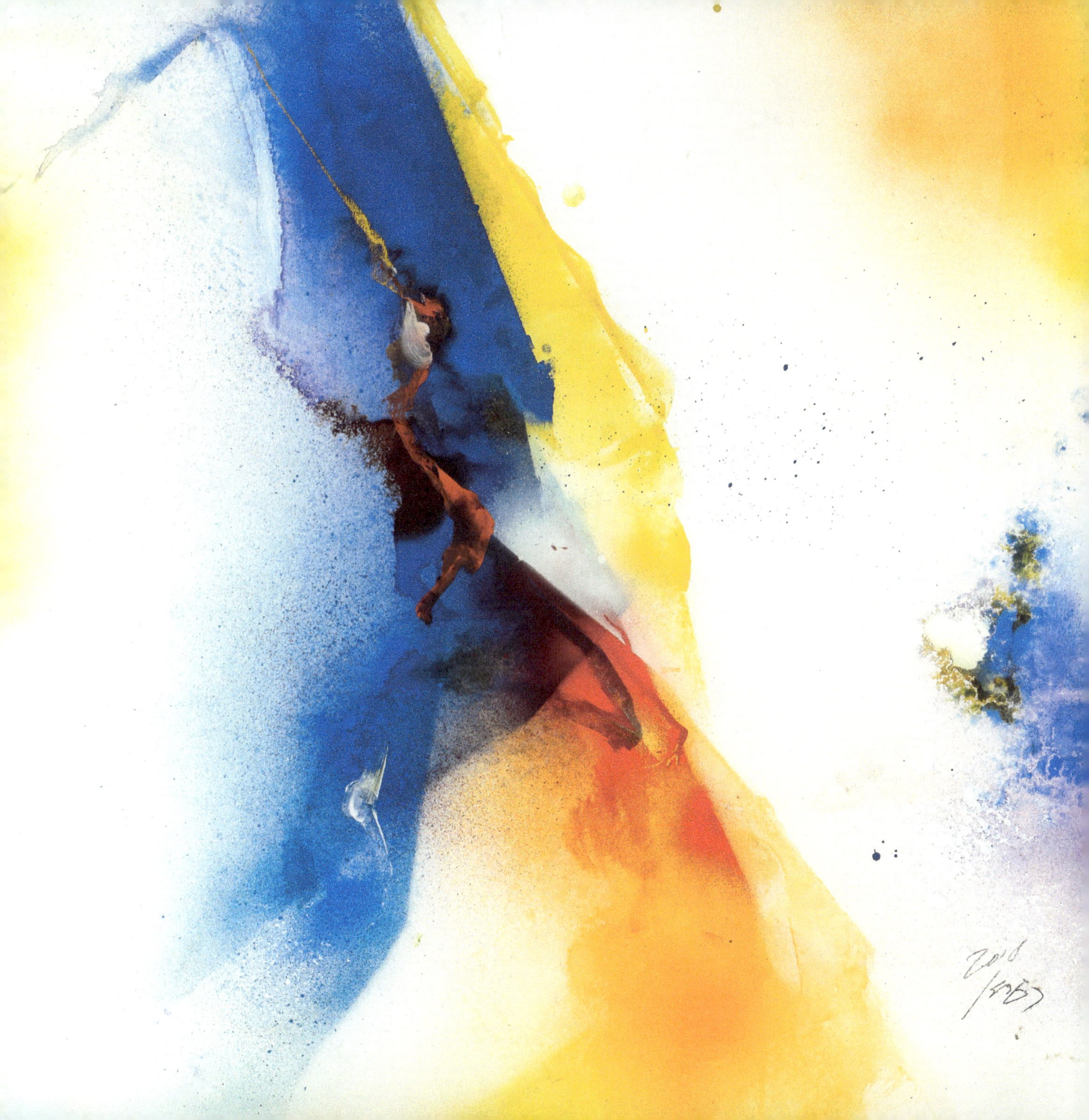

. . . the more we want to love God, the more we will want to understand who it is we love. The more we understand, the deeper our faith, the more absolute our love.[35]

35. *On Prayer*, 121.

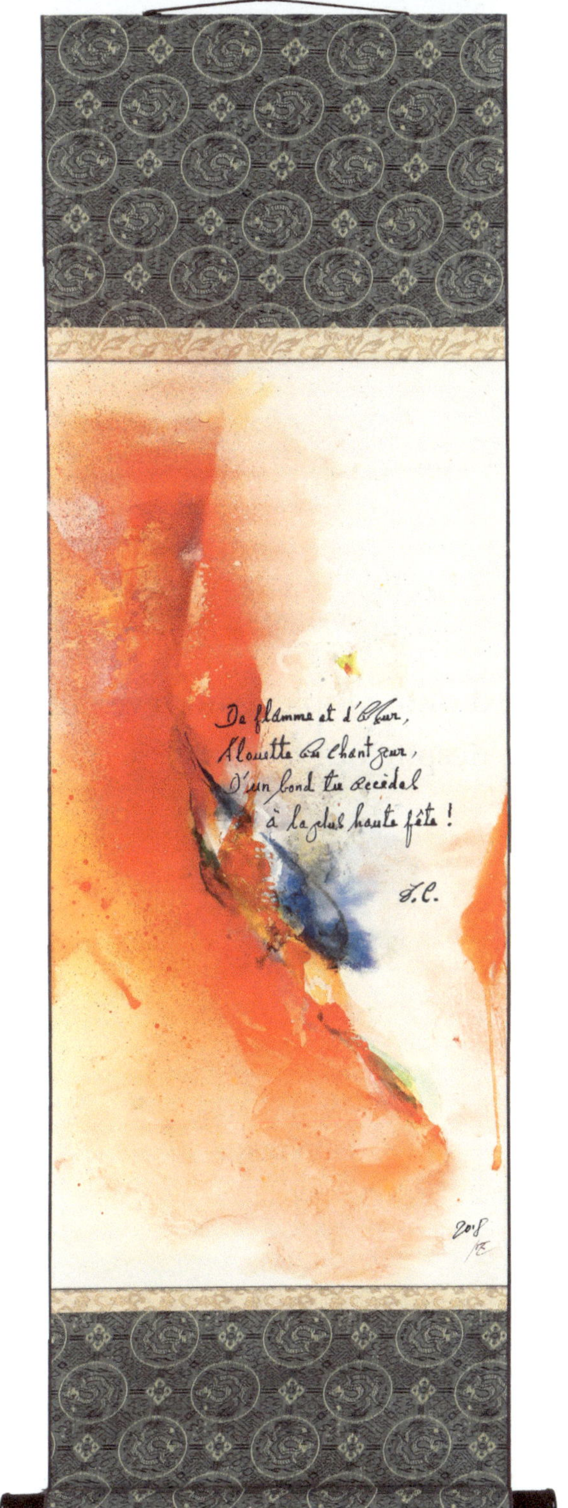

De flamme et d'azur,
Alouette au chant pur,
D'un bond tu accèdes
à la plus haute fête !
J.C.
2018

This is always the subtext of the Bible: God revealing his love, almost despite our actions.[36]

36. *Sister Wendy's Bible Treasury*, 26.

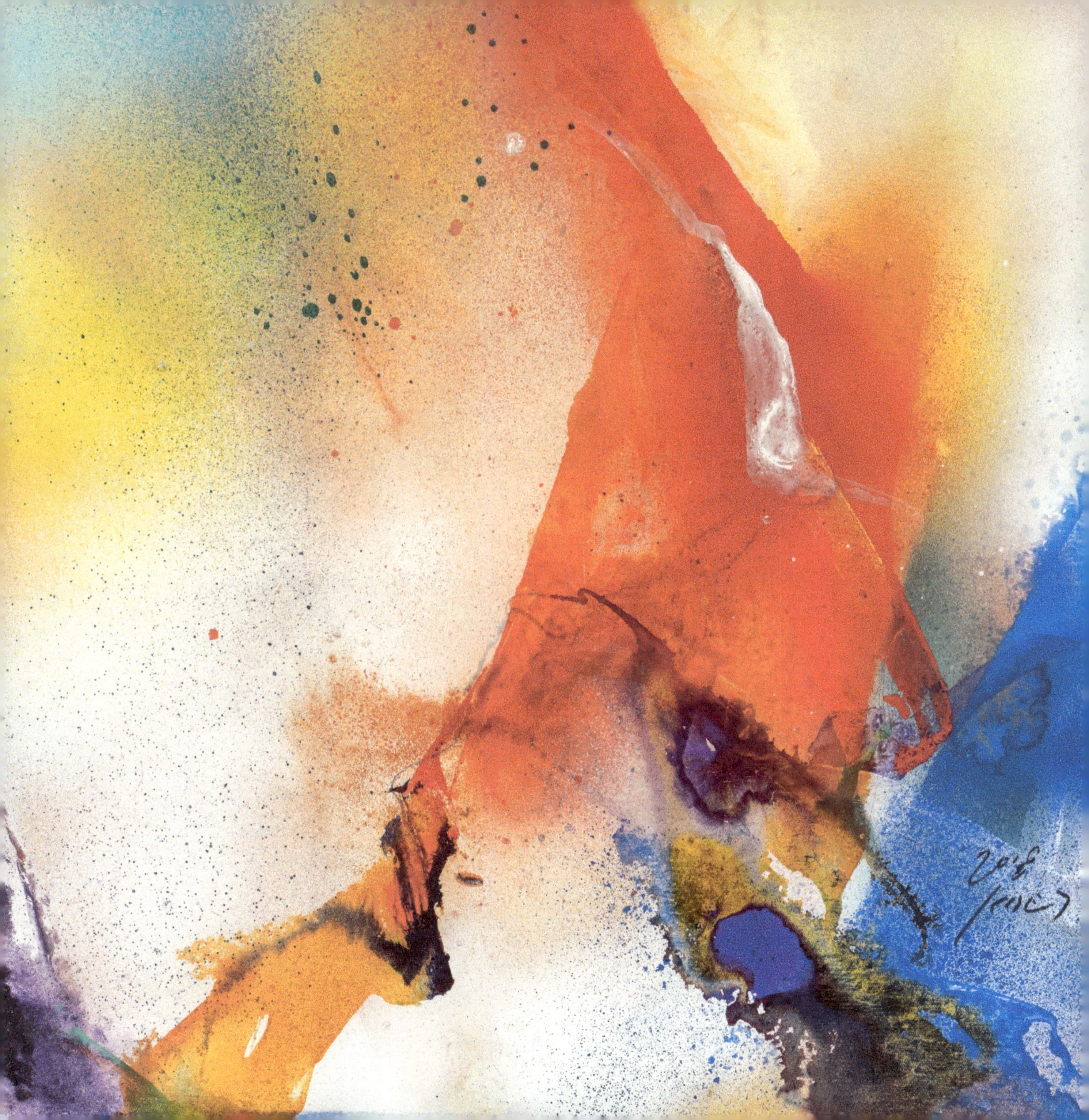

Autumn is the harvest time, and it is a wonderful stage for us to affirm our complete faith that God is our 'Harvest'. We have no home we've built, no career, no work—not even a spiritual achievement. We come to the end . . . with empty hands, and *glad* to have them empty, so that God can fill them . . .[37]

37. *Spiritual Letters*, 286.

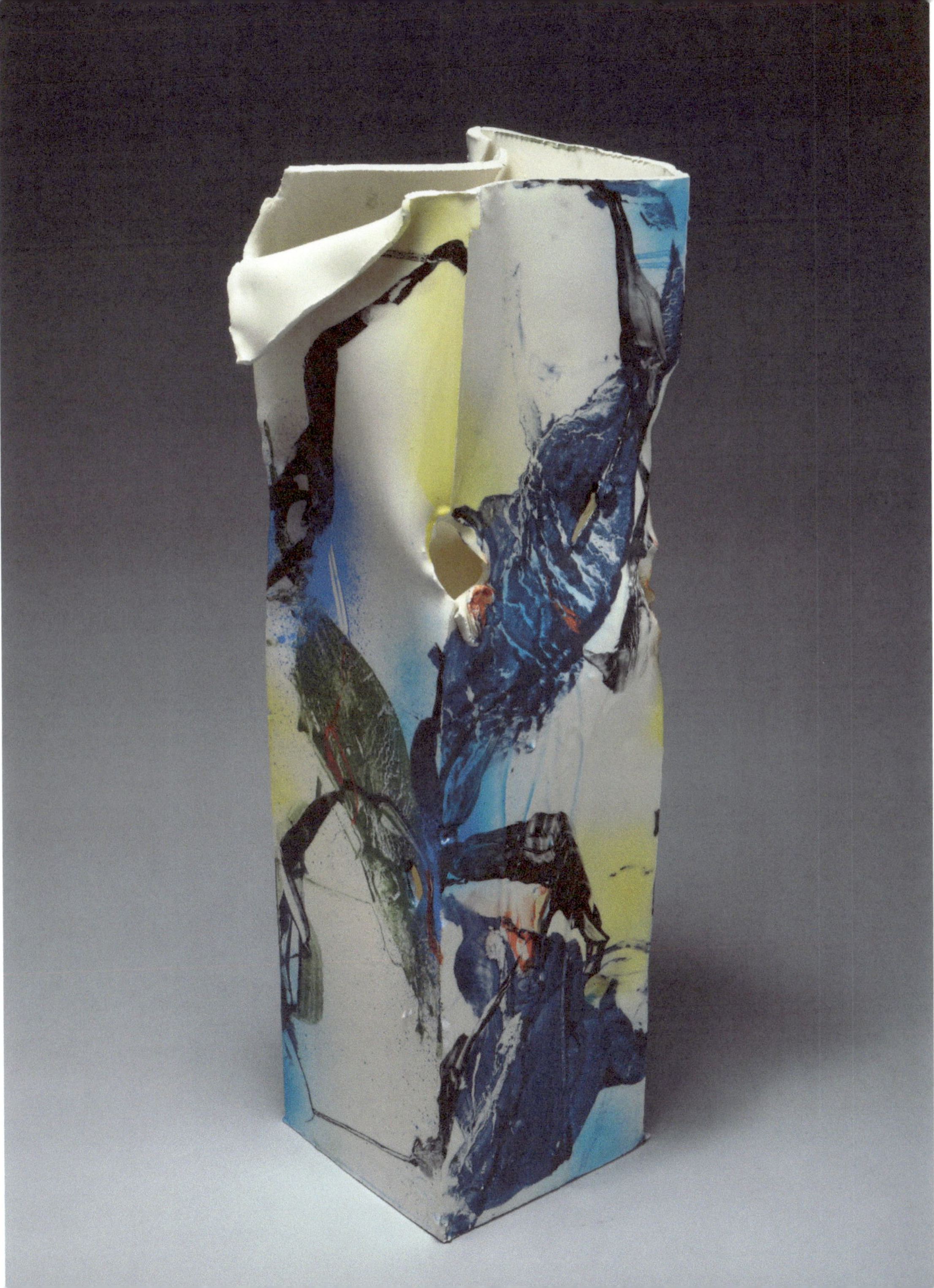

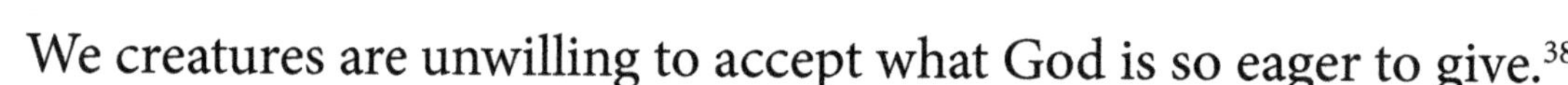

We creatures are unwilling to accept what God is so eager to give.[38]

38. *Sister Wendy's Bible Treasury*, 2.

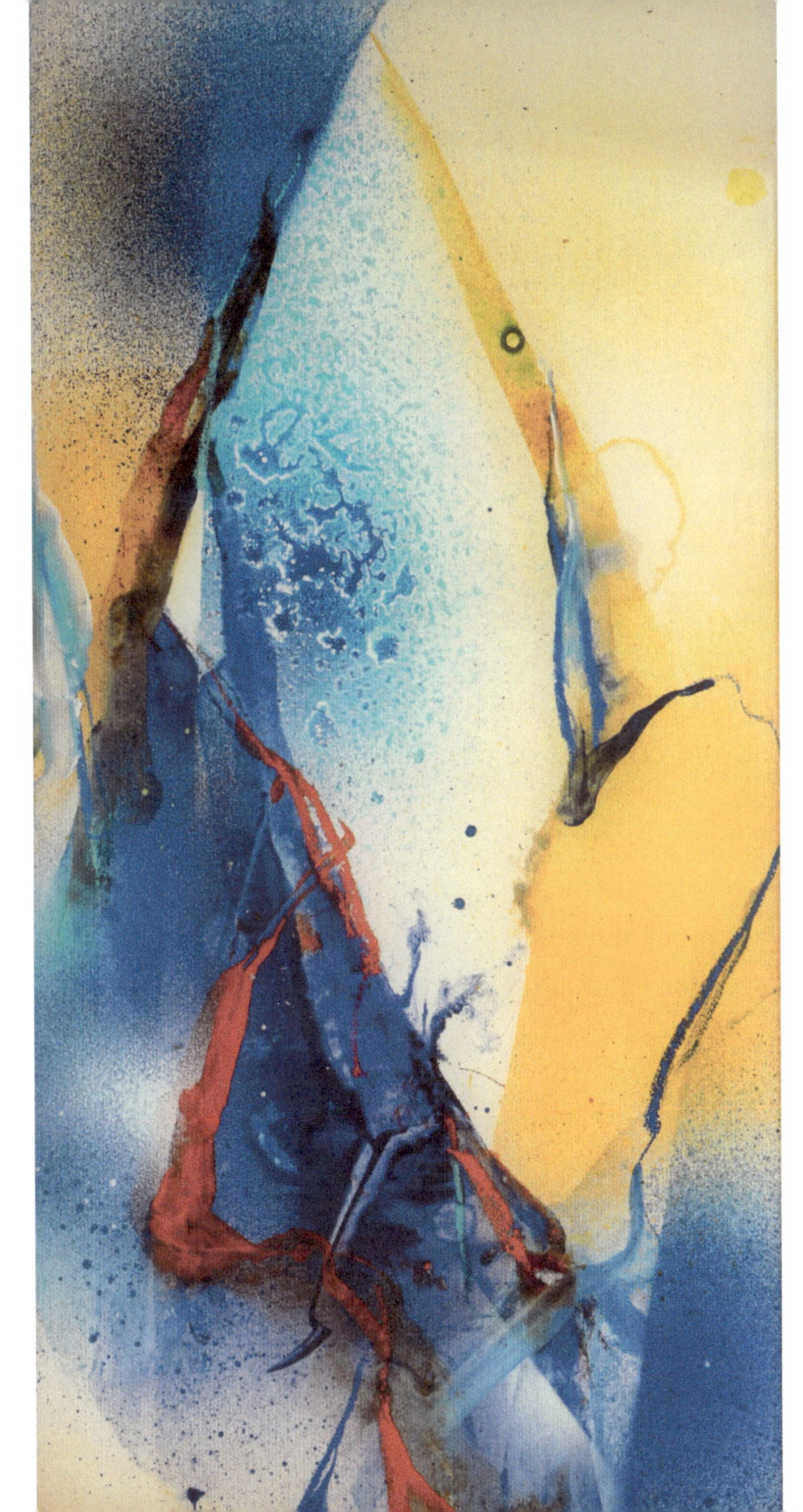

. . . I often say that we must receive God as He comes to us, that it's in the actual context of what-is that we find him . . .[39]

39. *Spiritual Letters*, 270.

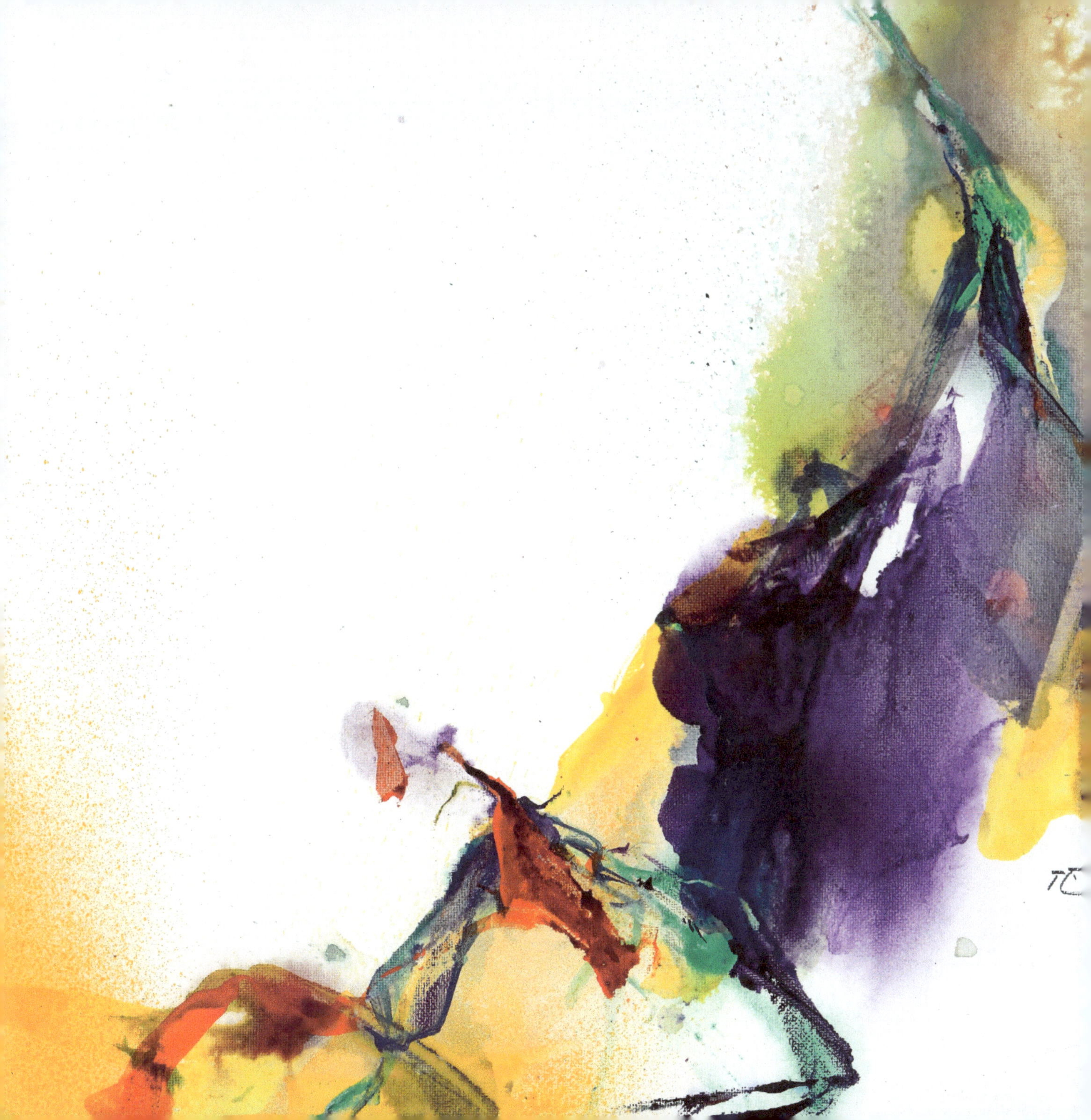

These stories [in the Bible] have a symbolic significance; they are showing us how God will use all circumstances, bad as well as good, to reach an end that will be of universal value.[40]

40. *Sister Wendy's Bible Treasury*, 51.

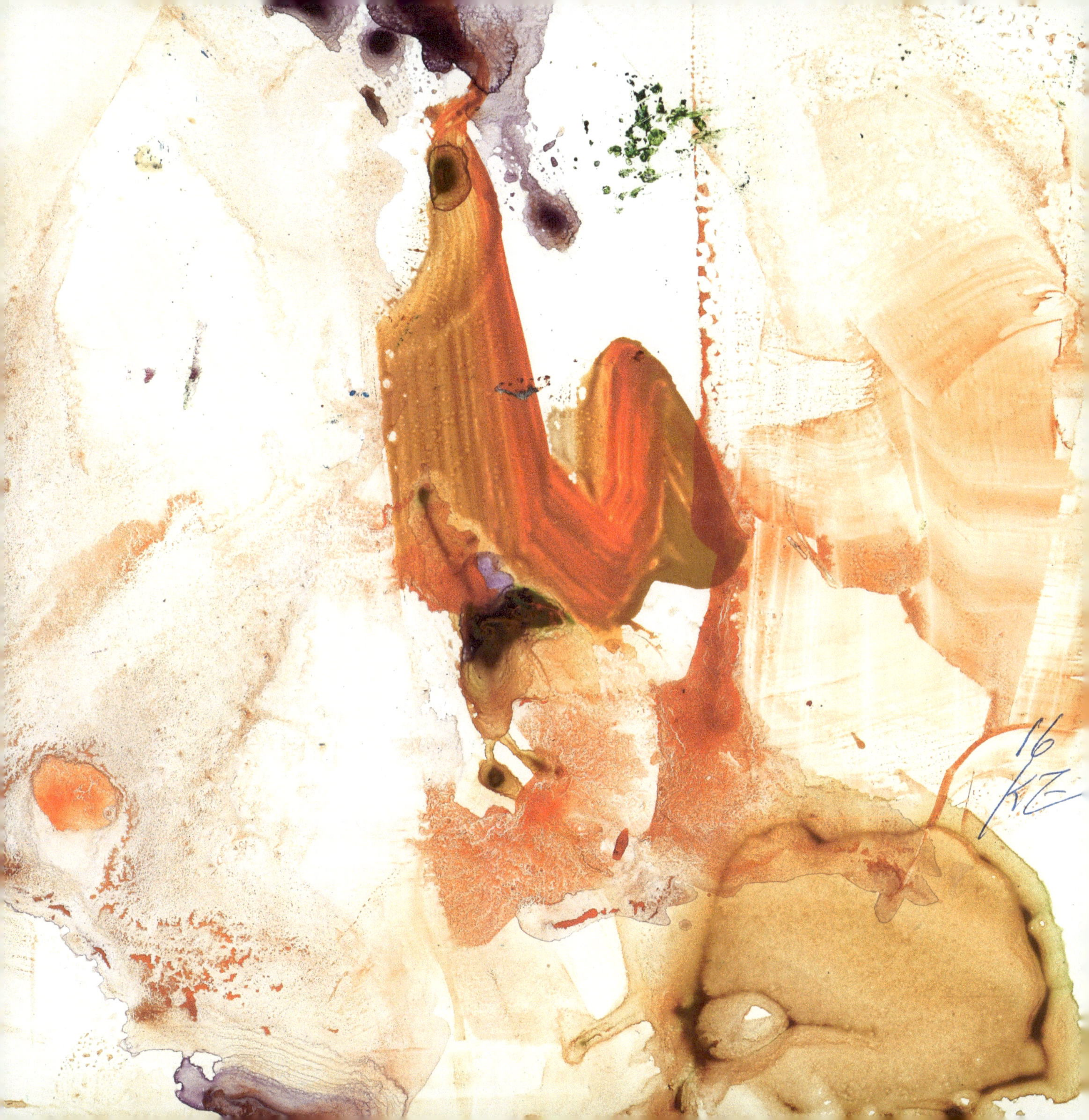
16
KZ

In homage of the following artists

Vincent van Gogh
Franz Klein
Willem de Koning
Marc Chagall
Francisco Goya
Rembrandt
Sandro Botticelli
Ferdinand Victor Eugène Delacroix
Giotto di Bondone
Albert Charles Herbert
Saint Francis
Ricardo Morandi
Rogier van der Weyden
Jordan Asher Cruz (Boots)
Pablo Picasso
El Greco
Andrey Rublev
Mark Rothko
Fra Angelico
Michelangelo Merisi da Caravaggio
Peter Paul Rubens
Raffaello Sanzio da Urbino (Raphael)
Angelica Kauffman
Paul Cézanne
Annibale Carracci
Artemisia Gentileschi
Dan Witz
Edgar Degas
Diego Rodríguez de Silva y Velázquez
Nicolas Poussin
Parmigiano-Reggiano
Pierre Soulages
Hieronymus Bosch
Gabriel Orozco
Pierre Bonnard

Lightning Source UK Ltd.
Milton Keynes UK
UKHW050902270520
363886UK00001B/13